BUSINESS LOAN COSTS AND BANK MARKET STRUCTURE

BUSINESS LOAN COSTS
and BANK MARKET STRUCTURE:
An Empirical Estimate
of Their Relations

DONALD P. JACOBS

NORTHWESTERN UNIVERSITY

OCCASIONAL PAPER 115

NEW YORK 1971

NATIONAL BUREAU OF ECONOMIC RESEARCH

DISTRIBUTED BY *Columbia University Press, New York & London*

PRINTED IN THE UNITED STATES OF AMERICA

ISBN 0-87014-239-9

1. The object of the National Bureau of Economic Research is to ascertain and to present to the public important economic facts and their interpretation in a scientific and impartial manner. The Board of Directors is charged with the responsibility of ensuring that the work of the National Bureau is carried on in strict conformity with this object.

2. The President of the National Bureau shall submit to the Board of Directors, or to its Executive Committee, for their formal adoption all specific proposals for research to be instituted.

3. No research report shall be published until the President shall have submitted to each member of the Board the manuscript proposed for publication, and such information as will, in his opinion and in the opinion of the author, serve to determine the suitability of the report for publication in accordance with the principles of the National Bureau. Each manuscript shall contain a summary drawing attention to the nature and treatment of the problem studied, the character of the data and their utilization in the report, and the main conclusions reached.

4. For each manuscript so submitted, a special committee of the Board shall be appointed by majority agreement of the President and Vice Presidents (or by the Executive Committee in case of inability to decide on the part of the President and Vice Presidents), consisting of three directors selected as nearly as may be one from each general division of the Board. The names of the special manuscript committee shall be stated to each Director when the manuscript is submitted to him. It shall be the duty of each member of the special manuscript committee to read the manuscript. If each member of the manuscript committee signifies his approval within thirty days of the transmittal of the manuscript, the report may be published. If at the end of that period any member of the manuscript committee withholds his approval, the President shall then notify each member of the Board, requesting approval or disapproval of publication, and thirty days additional shall be granted for this purpose. The manuscript shall then not be published unless at least a majority of the entire Board who shall have voted on the proposal within the time fixed for the receipt of votes shall have approved.

5. No manuscript may be published, though approved by each member of the special manuscript committee, until forty-five days have elapsed from the transmittal of the report in manuscript form. The interval is allowed for the receipt of any memorandum of dissent or reservation, together with a brief statement of his reasons, that any member may wish to express; and such memorandum of dissent or reservation shall be published with the manuscript if he so desires. Publication does not, however, imply that each member of the Board has read the manuscript, or that either members of the Board in general or the special committee have passed on its validity in every detail.

6. Publications of the National Bureau issued for informational purposes concerning the work of the Bureau and its staff, or issued to inform the public of activities of Bureau staff, and volumes issued as a result of various conferences involving the National Bureau shall contain a specific disclaimer noting that such publication has not passed through the normal review procedures required in this resolution. The Executive Committee of the Board is charged with review of all such publications from time to time to ensure that they do not take on the character of formal research reports of the National Bureau, requiring formal Board approval.

7. Unless otherwise determined by the Board or exempted by the terms of paragraph 6, a copy of this resolution shall be printed in each National Bureau publication.

(Resolution adopted October 25, 1926, and revised February 6, 1933, February 24, 1941, and April 20, 1968)

CONTENTS

TABLES

ACKNOWLEDGMENTS

THIS STUDY was financed by a grant from the American Bankers Association to the National Bureau. In addition to financing, the American Bankers Association and especially Charls E. Walker, the Executive Vice President, and Thomas R. Atkinson, former director of the Association's Department of Economic Research, were crucially important in developing the body of data which distinguishes this from preceding studies of the same topic. A large number of bank officers spent considerable time supplying the data requested in the questionnaire. The help of all these bankers is gratefully acknowledged.

The National Bureau staff reading committee, consisting of David T. Kresge, Michael Gort, Jack M. Guttentag, Robert P. Shay, and Lawrence Miller, made a number of helpful comments on an earlier draft of the manuscript. I would also like to thank Atherton Bean, Walter E. Hoadley, and Kelvin J. Lancaster, the National Bureau Board Reading Committee. Useful criticisms were also given by Charles Haywood and Eugene Lerner.

Keypunching of data from the questionnaire was done at the National Bureau under the supervision of Martha Jones. The large volume of computer data manipulation was done at Northwestern's Vogelback Computer Center with the assistance of Leland Brendsel and George Sherling. Virginia Meltzer edited the manuscript.

Chapter 1

THE STUDY, ITS RATIONALE AND PLAN

IN A free enterprise economy, such as exists in the United States, there is a widespread belief in the ability of competition and the price mechanism to produce efficient firm and market performance. However, some industries are subjected to substantial regulation. This usually occurs when the industry cost structure precludes reliance upon competition to produce efficient performance; a sufficient number of firms are not expected to survive in the unregulated environment for competition to ensue. Hence, price and/or output is subjected to governmental constraints.

The commercial banking industry purchases a wide variety of factor inputs and produces a broad array of products. These operations are subjected to a heavy framework of regulations; the rationale being their crucial role in the creation of the nation's money stock, their central position in business financing, their control over the transfer mechanism which handles the vast majority of money payments, and the fact that they are entrusted with a large fraction of the liquid funds in the economy. The goals that prompt bank regulations are not necessarily dominated by the desire for efficiency. Even if it is determined that regulation of banking operations is desirable, it is necessary to know what effect a regulation or combination of regulations has on economic efficiency. Such information is needed because the cost in efficiency of a particular regulation or set of regulations may be found to be greater than the expected social benefits; there are possible tradeoffs between goals and alternative regulations which would be desired; or the combination of regulations may be altered to achieve the desired policy goals with a smaller impact on economic efficiency.

When an individual firm operates in a market that is not perfectly competitive and faces a downward sloping demand curve, less is produced and the price is higher than under perfectly competitive conditions. Because of the relatively small number of competing banks in most markets, the wide range of products supplied, and the great potential for differentiating ostensibly similar products, there is no possibility that bank markets conform to the classical description of competitive markets. However, most banks do operate subject to substantial competitive pressure from other banks and from other suppliers of similar services. The degree of competition varies among markets and even within markets for different products. It is clear that the products where banks face lower competitive pressure will have higher prices and less product sales than would occur if competition were more intense. What is not clear, however, is the intensity of competition that prevails in bank markets and the extent of the differences in competitive vigor between bank markets that are attributable to structural differences induced by regulations.

Among the set of banking regulations, branching restrictions are the most pervasively influential in determining the structure of banking markets. Other regulations, such as restrictions on entry and restriction on payments for deposits, have a less important effect on structure. The number of banks in a market is a positive function and the number of bank offices in a bank market is a negative function of the degree of branching restriction, although there is some question of whether these functional relationships are linear.[1] Concentration is negatively

---

[1] There are three distinct classes of branching restrictions: branching permitted statewide, branching restricted within some part of the state, and complete prohibition of branches. The question of linearity arises with respect to whether the restricted branching states lie between the unit and statewide branching states with regard to both offices and banks. For a discussion of the problems of estimating these relationships and the differences in estimates, see Donald P. Jacobs, "The Interaction Effects of Restrictions on Branching and Other Bank Regulations," *Journal of Finance*, May 1965, pp. 332–348;

related to the number of banks in the market, and, therefore, it is also a negative function of the degree of branching restriction.

Economic theory suggests that the level of concentration of an industry's assets influences the competitive condition of the market but economic theory does not provide an analytical solution to the relative tradeoff in competitive intensity between the higher number of offices and the lower number of banks. Neither does economic theory provide an answer to the question of the size of the impact of concentration on price. Moreover, neither economic nor organizational theory provide any insight into whether differences in the organizational composition of banks in the market because of branching restrictions has an impact on the intensity of competition and, therefore, on prices charged. Thus, the question of the relationship between market structure and performance can, for the most part, only be answered empirically.

This study attempts to supply an empirical estimate of the relationship of market structure to the performance of banks in supplying services to businesses. It aims to provide an answer to the question: What is the relationship between market structure variables and the price businesses pay banks for services provided? It should be noted that this is only part of the larger question of the relationship of market structure to the performance of banks. But, since the provision of services to businesses encompasses a major portion of the totality of services provided by banks, the conclusions will have considerable relevance to the larger question.

Chapter 2 is devoted to developing models from which the parameters of the price-structure relationship can be estimated. These models must be based upon a description of how banks price their services to businesses. The procedure is to first develop a bank pricing model. The pricing model is then

---

Bernard Shull and Paul M. Horvitz, "Branch Banking and Structure of Competition," *National Banking Review*, March 1964, pp. 301–341; R.F. Lanzillotti and T.R. Saving, "State Branching Restrictions and the Availability of Branching Services," *Journal of Money, Credit, and Banking*, November 1969, pp. 778–788.

modified to a form that allows parameter estimates of the price-structure relationship.

A major implication of the pricing model is that, if maximization of discounted long-run profits is the goal of bank management, prices of individual products will be set to make a profit on the package of services provided to a customer. The observed prices of individual products is affected by the package of services purchased by the customer. A correct specification of the price of bank services must, therefore, take into account all products and services contained in the price or prices paid by a customer.[2] Estimating an equation constructed on the basis of bank customers requires data that represent the entire profile of a customer's relationship at a bank.

A second important implication of the model is that business customers compensate banks with three types of payments: interest on loans, deposit balances, and fees. At this time the first two of these account for the vast majority of bank compensation; fees are relatively unimportant. Therefore, both interest rates and deposit balances must be taken into account in any conclusions about the impact of market structure on the price businesses pay for bank services.

All prior studies of the price-market structure relationship in banking specified models that stipulated the interest rate on loans as the only price, and size of loan and possibly loan term as the services provided. Data availability was a major reason behind these model specifications; data describing other customer characteristics were simply not available.

To develop the data required to estimate the parameters of the price-structure relationship, a questionnaire was sent to a sample of over 600 banks with assets between \$40 and \$400

[2] The description and analysis of bank pricing practices has prompted a large volume of research. The hypothesis that bank pricing can be rationalized if the bank is viewed as establishing a long-term relationship with its business customers, which is the central theme of the pricing model developed in the next chapter, was first formulated and analyzed by Donald R. Hodgman in his pioneering study, *Commercial Bank Loan and Investment Policy*, Bureau of Economics and Business Research, University of Illinois, Champaign, 1963.

million at the end of 1966.[3] Banks in the $40-$60 million asset class were requested to supply 40 customer profiles; those in the $80-$120 million asset class were asked for 60 customer profiles; and banks in the $200-$400 million class were asked for 80 customer profiles. Replies were received from 160 banks with data covering approximately 8,500 customers.[4] The responding banks include the three classes of branching restrictions and have a large variance in market size and measured concentration of deposits.

The asset size range of banks included in the sample was chosen with the study in mind. It is believed that if market structure does influence performance, the relationship would be most evident and easily measured in the prices paid by customers in banks of these sizes. The pricing decisions of smaller banks would be expected to contain such a large amount of nonsystematic elements that the noise level would make valid measurement very difficult. On the other hand, larger banks, because they operate in a national market, have a substantial portion of their business transactions subjected to competitive forces outside of their local bank market. Hence, data from these banks would, in the main, not reflect the local market conditions that this study attempts to isolate.

In Chapter 3, the parameters of two basic models, one with loan price and the other with deposit balances as the dependent variable, are estimated. The main emphasis of the chapter is on the analysis and interpretation of the parameter estimates of the structural variables; whether these variables are statistically significant and, if they are, upon their signs and sizes. This analysis leads to conclusions, in the fourth chapter, about the quantitative importance of differences in bank market structure and the direction of influence on the level of bank prices.

[3] The questionnaire is reproduced as Appendix A.
[4] The location and class size of responding banks and a description of the questions and responses to the questionnaire are included in Appendix B.

A MODEL TO ESTIMATE PRICE
DIFFERENCES BETWEEN MARKETS

THE BANK PRICING PROCESS

TO ESTIMATE the effect of market structure on the prices business customers are charged, it is necessary to understand how banks price their services. A pricing model for business services cannot properly be developed in isolation from the other activities of the bank. Strategies for pricing services and determining how many and which services to supply businesses are affected by the total set of opportunities that face the bank and the total set of resources available to the bank. The development of a strategy for pricing business services in this framework requires a model which treats the entire banking firm as a system, but a formal systems model of the bank is beyond the scope of this study.[1] It will be necessary, however, to at least describe the salient features of such a model to develop the required insights

---

[1] It is worth noting that a number of large banks have developed linear programming (LP) models as a solution algorithm for a similar but somewhat narrower set of decisions. These models have been designed to guide bank asset allocation decisions taking into account the capital constraint under which banks operate. Two examples in the literature of such models are D. Chambers and A. Charnes, "Intertemporal Analysis and Optimization of Bank Portfolios," *Management Science*, July 1961; and K. J. Cohen and F. S. Hammer, "Linear Programming and Optimal Bank Asset Management Decisions," *Journal of Finance*, May 1967. Although these LP models are prototypes of similar models that have been used by banks to make decisions, this chapter contends that they have misspecified the true constraints under which banks operate. Equity capital is not the constrained resource; rather it will be argued that the constraint is liquidity during periods of tight monetary conditions and the requirement that banks meet loan commitments to customers during such periods.

for studying the effects of structure on the bank's pricing strategies.

It can be hypothesized that a bank's pricing decisions begin with the specification of goals. A banker, like other entrepreneurs, may be motivated by a number of objectives. It is assumed, however, that as a single goal the banker strives to maximize the discounted value of the bank's income stream over a planning horizon. If other goals exist, the strategy described could be modified to take these into account. It is further assumed that banks are risk averters, which means the banker must be compensated for any increase in risk. Moreover, the risk aversion of bankers is relatively stronger than that of most other business managers because of the low capital ratios maintained by banks and because of the emphasis bank examiners place on loss experience as an index of the quality of management. This high degree of risk aversion is, therefore, an extremely influential element in the pricing and asset decisions of banks.

Like other firms, a bank begins with an endowment of equity. It purchases raw materials and utilizes a production function to convert these raw materials into products which it sells. Given this description, a major difference between a bank and most other enterprises is the fact that bank decisions in the factor and product markets are circumscribed by regulatory prohibitions.

The most important regulatory constraint on the pricing strategy of banks is the prohibition of interest payments on demand deposits. Deposits are a basic raw material in their production function; hence, banks must develop strategies to compete for these deposits, usually by lowering the price of services rendered to compensate the customer for the value of deposits. Since business customers purchase a wide range of bank products and need deposits for transactions, they can be enticed to keep deposits balances wherever they are reimbursed most satisfactorily. Thus, the bank and the business customer typically develop a relationship in which bartering is an important component. The prices of individual bank products are influenced by the deposit balance of the purchaser. But business customers use a variety of products and all prices should not be reduced to take account of the same deposits. Since the typical bank is organized by departments along product lines, a customer pricing algorithm must be developed to provide information to individual departments of the banks on how much to offset its prices on the products it provides.

This implies that the prohibition of interest on demand deposits has forced banks to develop a pricing policy for the total customer package rather than for each of its products independently. However, there are good reasons to believe that a package pricing policy would have developed in the absence of this regulation and would continue if it is abolished. Individual banks sell a wide range of products such as check transfer, loans, trust and pension administration, stock transfer, data processing services, etc., with varying demand elasticities and, hence, varying profit margins on individual business customers. It is reasonable to believe banks would find it desirable to offset the prices of products where the bank faces low demand elasticities in order to entice customers to purchase other products with a higher elasticity of demand.[2] Since the lending arrangement is the major focus for the business customer, the bank takes account of profitable sales of its other products to the customer in determining the loan price or other prices in the package of services provided. This is especially the case where there is a high probability the customer will shift all purchases if he is enticed to switch the source of one of the services. Thus, it is the nature of the customer-bank relationship that forces a customer pricing policy. The bank will continue to serve the customer if it believes him to be profitable over the long run or planning horizon.

The need to accommodate the loan demand of profitable customers, at the request of the customer, imposes opportunity

---

[2] This is the traditional tied-sale strategy. For a discussion of the economies of the tied-sale, see Meyer L. Burstein, "The Economics of Tie-in Sales," *Review of Economics and Statistics*, February 1960, pp. 68–73.

costs on the bank. In general, the loan offer, which is often an implicit rather than explicit part of the relationship, is made subject to the prime bank rate which will exist when the loan is requested. During periods of easy money, the bank can validate its loan commitments because of the interindustry variation in the seasonal demand for loans by its business customers, or if an unexpectedly large demand develops, it can easily acquire additional funds at reasonable prices relative to the loan rate.

During periods of tight money, interindustry differences in seasonal loan demands break down as higher than usual proportions of customer request loans. In such periods, the marginal cost of acquiring additional funds is relatively high compared to easy money periods and the supply schedule of funds to any individual bank becomes less elastic. The existence of Regulation Q intensifies the potential problem a bank faces in acquiring external funds during tight money periods by making the supply schedule even less elastic than it would otherwise be. Because the prime bank rate is sticky, the spread between loan rates and purchased money costs declines and at times becomes negative. Banks suffer large actual and/or opportunity losses on loans to customers with whom they have profitable long-run relationships. To reduce opportunity losses, the bank can maintain assets which can be easily liquidated to meet the higher loan demand. But, liquidity has a lower opportunity cost during periods of easy money conditions. Thus, the bank must develop a liquidity strategy based on the level of profits versus losses it is willing to accept in easy or tight money periods.

To be profitable, the customer must compensate the bank for the costs entailed in the loan commitment. Banks have exhibited a strong desire to receive this compensation in the form of deposit balances. This is explained by the high degree of risk aversion of bank management due to low capital ratios. The loan commitment to customers who are expected to be profitable over the planning horizon imposes the major risk undertaken by the bank. During periods of tight money, the high cost of funds to meet such commitments could lead to substantial losses. Compensating deposits are the main source of deposits at an assured price during periods of tight money. They can, therefore, be viewed as a reciprocal insurance premium. On the one hand, they are a payment from the customer to the bank to assure the granting of loan requests; on the other hand, the bank accepts a lower payment in deposits rather than cash fees to lower its risk exposure.

A CUSTOMER PROFITABILITY MODEL

A customer's expected profitability to a bank for a single period of time can be expressed as follows:[3]

$$\pi_i = L_i(R_{iL} - R_A - R_{iR}) - C_{iL} + D_i(1 - rr)R_A - Y_iA + \sum_{j=1}^{N} S_{ij}, \quad (1)$$

where π_i represents the dollars of profit from the ith customer during period t; L_i, the loan balance of the ith customer during period t; R_{iL}, the loan rate for the ith customer's loan during period t; R_A, the bank's cost of acquiring a dollar of lendable funds during period t; R_{iR}, the probability that the ith customer will default on the loan during period t; C_{iL}, the cost of making the ith customer loan, including credit search and handling costs; D_i, the mean deposit balance of the ith customer for period t; rr, the reserve requirement on demand deposits; Y_i, the change in average yield on assets during period t, because of liquidity addition resulting from the loan commitment entailed by the ith customer relationship; A, the total assets of the bank during period t; and S_{ij}, the fees received for providing the jth type of service for the ith customer during period t, minus the costs incurred in providing the service.

The expression $L_i\ (R_{iL} - R_A - R_{iR}) - C_{iL}$ represents the net

[3] The customer profit formulation is presented in this manner because of the estimation requirements of the study. A bank decision framework would call for the development of a linear, chance constrained, or dynamic programming model. The bank maximizes the discounted value of its income stream given its demand schedule, supply schedule, and production. Moreover, it operates subject to a policy decision on the quantity of risk management will accept, which is the probability of liquidity costs, losses on liquidating securities, and opportunity losses due to the need to purchase high cost money to meet loan requests during periods of tight money conditions.

revenue expected from the loan component of the customer relationship. The R_{iL} is the real rate implied by the loan contract. Because of repayment clauses or interest prepayment clauses this may be different from the rate stipulated in the contract.

In principle, the R_A term should not be the marginal cost of funds during the one period t, but should be evaluated after taking into account all alternatives available to the bank through the planning horizon.[4] R_A is also the opportunity cost of funds to the bank. Even if two banks have identical cost of funds schedules, in terms of payments made to external suppliers, they may have different R_A terms because of variations in the opportunities they face in using their available funds. The R_A term is really the shadow price or dual variable of lendable funds when this problem is viewed in a mathematical programming format. Since all banks face identical supply schedules in the securities market, differences in opportunities are functions of the loan markets. Banks in different markets have varying loan demands because of strong or weak savings and loan or mutual savings bank competition for mortgages, variations in the competitive fervor of sales finance and small loan companies for consumer loans, and the intensity of competition from other banks in the business lending sphere. The difference in the R_A term will produce measured differences in the π_i between markets, if market structure is related to the prices businesses are charged for services.

In banking, it is usual to think of the R_{iR} term as the difference between the prime rate and the rate charged. This simplistic view of bank pricing is countered by the concept of a customer

[4] This is the problem that arises in capital budgeting when the firm faces an upward sloping cost of capital. If the entire set of projects available through the planning horizon is not included in the analysis, projects evaluated at an early point in the decision process face a lower cost of capital than those at a later point. Because of this simultaneous solution process, an optimum decision can only be made when all investment alternatives and the cost of funds schedules, through the planning horizon, are viewed concurrently. This problem is also solved by a linear programming solution algorithm; see William J. Baumol and Richard E. Quandt, "Investment and Discount Rates Under Capital Rationing: A Programming Approach," *The Economic Journal,* June 1965, pp. 317–329.

relationship where the price of any product cannot be isolated from the other prices in the package. In this formulation, it is assumed that the sum of R_{iR} payments just compensates the bank for losses experienced. Thus, this sum is subtracted from the net revenue expected from borrowing customers.

The C_{iL} term includes both the direct costs incurred in processing the loan forms and monitoring the loan agreement during the periods in which loans to the ith customer are out-standing and also the costs incurred in monitoring the credit position of the customer when loans are not outstanding. Thus, this term has a positive value for all borrowing customers during all periods.

In any period, therefore, the expression $L_i (R_{iL} - R_A - R_{iR})$ $- C_{iL}$ could have a positive or negative contribution to profits. When loans are outstanding during periods of monetary ease, this component of the relationship almost always produces a positive contribution. A rare exception could occur where the lending component of the relationship is very small relative to deposits maintained or where the customer purchases other profitable products, causing the bank to make loans at unusually low rates. During periods of tight money, a negative value could occur for a large number of customers. During such periods it is not unusual for R_A to be greater than R_{iL}.

The term $D_i (1 - rr) R_A$ represents the value received from the customer's deposit balance. Reserves must be subtracted from deposits to determine balances available to the bank. The appropriateness of using only the single parameter, average balance, to denote D_i is open to some question because of the value a bank puts on the certainty of having the deposit when required. It may be desirable to add a penalty term for wide variations within the period. Using R_A as a measure of the value of a dollar of demand deposit balances held by borrowing cus-tomers probably understates the true worth of these deposits. They have a high probability of being available during periods of peak needs and are, therefore, more valuable, on the average, than funds derived from more volatile sources.

The term $Y_i A$, which is the change in revenue from the bank's assets not including revenues from the ith customer's loans, accounts for the cost imposed on the bank in the form of a reduced return on assets because of the implicit or explicit commitment to accommodate the loan requests of the customer. During periods when the customer is borrowing the maximum amount the bank will loan, this term will be zero. The size of the sum of $Y_i A$ for the entire bank is determined by the amount of risk the bank management is willing to assume. Banks which have large YA costs will experience small losses due to high costs of purchased funds during periods of high loan demand, when tight money conditions prevail. The large YA cost is due to substantial holdings of short dated securities which provide liquidity but impose a penalty on the current period's revenue. Banks which have small amounts of such liquid assets will experience large losses during periods of peak loan demand. Such banks have invested funds not employed in loans in longer term investments, which cause capital losses during tight money periods, or they have high loan to deposit ratios during periods of easy money conditions and are required to purchase high cost funds or turn away good customers during periods of high loan demand.

The term $\sum_{j=1}^{N} S_{ij}$ represents the sum of fees received by the bank from the charges levied on the nonlending services performed for the ith customer during period t, minus the costs incurred in providing these services. Since deposit balances are often used to compensate the bank for these services, many customers, even large users of such services, will make small or even no payments of fees and the coefficients of the S_j's will often be negative.

It has been stressed that the bank is a long-run profit maximizer. Thus, for any period t, π_i could have a positive or negative coefficient and still the customer could be acceptable. To determine if a customer is expected to be profitable, the computed profits for all periods through the planning horizon must be discounted at an appropriate rate and summed. The present value of the stream of profits (*PV*) expected from the *i*th customer is then:

$$PV_i = \sum_{t=1}^{N} \frac{\pi_{it}}{(1 + K_i)} t, \tag{2}$$

where K is a discount factor which equates the value of money in different periods.

The appropriate discount rate to equate earnings in future periods to a present value is a subject of wide controversy. For our purposes, it is sufficient to note that long-run customer profitability cannot be determined by simply adding income streams across periods. Money has a time value. Income received in early periods can be utilized to earn additional returns. Moreover, funds available in different periods have varying values depending on the relative opportunities available during the period.

If it is assumed that the bank's criterion function is to maximize the value of its discounted long-run profits, equations 1 and 2 fit into a simple decision rule. If the present value of the discounted stream of expected earnings is positive, the customer should be served. If the stream is negative, the customer should be rejected.

If the model of bank pricing behavior developed in equations 1 and 2 describes pricing policies of banks, then it contains implications on how an empirical investigation of the relationship of bank market structure to prices charged must proceed. The model implies that profit maximizing decisions on whether or not to serve a customer are determined by an estimate of over-all customer profitability, which largely depends upon the net revenues from nonloan services the customer is expected to purchase and the expected cyclical distribution of the customer's loan demand and deposit balances. Observed individual prices may be affected by the profitability of other portions of the packages of services purchased by the customer. Potentially high profit customers are in a strong position to bargain for a reduction in the price of some individual products. If the customer's profitability is marginal, the bank is in a strong position to raise some individual product prices in the package of services performed.

When a package pricing concept is introduced, the question of price differences between markets is transformed into differences in the profitability at which customers will be accepted. But, even this relatively difficult formulation has been shown to inadequately describe the complexity of the problem. The profitability computation extends over a number of periods. A customer's total contribution could produce a loss in some periods and still have a positive expected value over the planning horizon. The experimental design suggested by equations 1 and 2 is not feasible for empirical estimation of market performance. It would be prohibitively expensive to collect data required to estimate customer profitability over an extended time period, for the necessary number of customers, distributed over the necessary range of market concentrations and types of branching restrictions, to determine if market structure affects customer profitability.

Because of the excessive data costs of a multiperiod model, it is necessary to develop a one-period model to estimate the market structure parameters. Equation 1, in isolation, is an example of such a model. It implies that the bank takes into account all of a customer's activities in a single period to determine profitability. In light of the model developed in both equations, which argued that profit maximizing decisions on acceptable customers should be predicated on expectations of a long-term profitable relationship, it is necessary to justify the use of parameters estimated from a one-period model. The usefulness of a one-period model depends upon a demonstration that biases are not introduced. The question of bias must be posed with regard to the purpose of the parameter estimates. One-period estimates would certainly not be reliable for profitability decisions by bank management, but this study is not involved in guiding individual bank decisions on profitable customer relationships. The customer models are designed to provide estimates of prices charged businesses for services in different bank markets as a starting point for an analysis of market structure effects. The question of bias then reduces to whether or not parameter estimates of the one-period model are related to structure variables differently than the parameters of the *N*-period model.

The parameter values of many of the elements of the customer relationship vector would be expected to change with cyclical phase. This is particularly true of the deposit balance and liquidity cost variables and least true of the estimates of net income derived from other services. But this study is not concerned with determining which customers should be served by a bank. Since all customers for whom we have data have been accepted for a relationship by a bank, for our purposes all that is required is that cyclical changes in the customer characteristic parameters not be influenced by market structure variations. Cyclical influences have a broad effect on the economy and have a differential impact on industries. Industries are to some degree concentrated regionally and bank market structure is also related to region, but there is no strong reason to believe that these relationships will introduce a bias into the empirical estimates. It is extremely unlikely that the industrial distribution of the sample of customers which was chosen in the set of SMSA's with one of the three types of branching restrictions is affected by the business cycle differently than the distribution of customers in the other two sets of SMSA's. It is concluded, therefore, that if banks price their business services to maximize long-run profits, a one-period model, such as equation 1, can be used to estimate the influence of market structure on profitability.

Since our interest is in prices charged rather than in customer profitability, and because some of the variables will be represented by a proxy because data are not available to measure them directly, equation 1 is restructured as follows:

$$R_L = B_1L + B_2D + B_3F + B_4T + B_5L_A + B_6A_A$$

$$+ B_7E + B_8S + \sum_{i=9}^{N} \sum_{j=1}^{M} B_iG_j + U, \quad (3)$$

where R_L, L, D, and S are defined as in equation 1; F is the fluctuation in depositor balances; T, the time in debt in months; L_A, the length of customer arrangement; A_A, the account activity; E, another bank; and G_j, variables depicting the individual bank, market demand, and market structure.

This model is similar to (1) in that it implies that the bank makes decisions based on a single period. The major difference is that the loan rate is assumed to be the major price which the bank uses to determine profitability of the customer. The net revenues received on other products in the package of services, the direct costs and opportunity costs entailed in the customer relationship, and the value of the deposits are assumed to influence the price charged for the loan.

In (3) the cost associated with the loan function and the risk assumed in lending to the customer are imbedded in the loan size variable, L. Other customer characteristics included in the model, such as deposit fluctuation, time in debt, length of customer arrangement, and account activity, are proxies for factors that influence the costs or revenues of the customer relationship that would be captured directly in the measured variables if equations 1 and 2 were estimated. These variables can be expected to influence the terms of the relationship in (1) and are, therefore, included.

The variables included in the G_j terms are proxies for R_A. Since this study was originally motivated by the desire to measure the parameters of the price-structure relationship, special interest is attached to the sign, size, and statistical significance of two of these variables, which will be a measure of concentration of ownership of deposits in the market and a dummy variable to capture the effect of branching restrictions. The YA term in equation 1 is deleted because there is no way to capture the effect of required liquidity for the individual customer.

The significance of equation 3, with loan rate designated as the crucial price of bank services, derives both from the fact that interest on loans is the major source of bank revenue and because loan rates have been used as the dependent variable in all other studies of the effect of market structure on price. Thus, the estimates derived from this model describe an important component of bank prices and can be compared to the findings of other studies.

For the purpose of this study, however, interest rates have a severe shortcoming because observed loan prices fluctuate within a very narrow range. Whatever the explanation for this, it is an observed fact that at the time of the customer survey interest rates on business loans were very rarely above 10 per cent or below the prime rate, which was 5.5 or 5.75 per cent. Moreover, the rates strongly cluster around 6 per cent (see column 2 in Table 1). The narrow range of the distribution of interest rates on business loans is not a manifestation of the particular set of banks and customers surveyed for this study, rather it is a general phenomenon of bank pricing. This same general distribution is found in many surveys of interest rates

TABLE 1.   Distribution of Business Loans by Interest Rates
(per cent)

Interest Rate (1)	Distribution of Number of Business Loans, Customer Sample (2)	Interest Rate (3)	Distribution of Dollar Amounts of Business Loans, February 1967 (4)	Distribution of Dollar Amounts of Business Loans, May 1967 (5)
<5.5	4.0	<5.5	2.0	2.1
5.5–5.99	39.0	5.5	3.1	32.1
6.0–6.49	29.3	5.51–6.0	57.1	35.4
6.5–6.99	20.4	6.01–6.49	13.3	11.2
7.0–7.49	3.7	6.5	5.9	5.5
7.5–7.99	2.3	6.51–6.99	7.1	4.8
8.0≤	1.3	7.0	5.0	3.8
		7.0 <	6.5	5.4

SOURCE: Column 2, National Bureau Survey of Bank Customer Profiles; columns 4 and 5, *Federal Quarterly Survey of Interest Rates, Federal Reserve Bulletin,* August 1967, p. 1392.

on loans for business purposes. Some examples are shown in columns 4 and 5 of Table 1. The two parts of Table 1, columns 1 and 2 and columns 3, 4, and 5, are more nearly identical than they at first appear. The customer profile data are unweighted; whereas, the Federal Reserve data are weighted by dollar amounts. Since larger loans have lower rates, the Federal Reserve survey should have a higher proportion than the customer profile in the lower rate brackets.

The narrow range of observed interest rates on business loans, coupled with the strong tendency to cluster around some "normal" rate and its extreme cyclical stickiness, strongly infers that the determination of the loan rate has a large non-systematic component. Discussions with bankers and the literature on bank management give the strong impression that rules of thumb and tradition play an important part in setting loan rates. Thus, there can be substantial movements in the independent variables that are not reflected in the loan rate. This is, of course, a problem of major concern for the empirical portions of this study and will be considerably elaborated in the next chapter.

The implication of equations 1 and 2 that banks are remunerated through three types of payments suggests that models similar to (3) should be formulated with deposit balances and fees designated as the dependent variable. But at this time fees are of relatively minor importance. Thus, only one additional equation will be constructed and estimated.

To measure the relationship of the deposit balance component of the vector of bank prices to market structure, equation 3 is reformulated as follows:

$$D = B_1L + B_2R_L + B_3F + B_4T + B_5L_A + B_6A_A$$
$$+ B_7E + B_8S + \sum_{i=9}^{N} \sum_{j=1}^{M} B_iG_j + U, \quad (4)$$

where all variables are defined as in (3).

This formulation of the model has much to commend it. The deposit balance is one of the most significant components of the customer-bank relationship. Conversations with bankers suggest that it is very often the crucial bargaining point of the relationship, particularly during periods of strong loan demand. Deposit balances impose a cost upon the business. Even if the balances are voluntarily held and there is increasing evidence that they are largely determined by bank compensation requirements, the business could bargain for additional bank services. Certainly, to the bank, the amount of balances maintained is an important component of the revenue received.

In the following chapter, the parameters of the variables in equations 3 and 4 will be estimated from the customer profile data collected for this study. The basic hypothesis of the study is that the prices of bank services paid by the business customers of banks are determined by components of the package of bank services purchased and the conditions of the banking market in which the customers are served. Thus, taking account of variations in customer profiles with regard to services used and differences in demand in the market, variations in the level of prices are attributed to market structure. The parameter values and the signs of the coefficients of the two structural variables will be analyzed to determine if prices are related to market structure and, if a relationship is established, to determine the quantitative importance of the structural variables on the level of prices businesses pay.

Chapter 3

STATISTICAL ESTIMATION OF THE PRICE-STRUCTURE RELATIONSHIP

INTRODUCTION

THE GOAL of this chapter is to determine through analysis of the parameter estimates of the market structure variables if there is a relationship between the interest price and/or the deposit price businesses pay banks for the services they purchase and the structure of bank markets. Before analyzing these statistical findings, however, it is desirable to rationalize the definition of banking markets used for the statistical tests and to make clear some of the problems that are introduced because of the use of a single-period model.

Delineating the geographic limits of a banking market is complicated by the large number of distinct products produced by banks. Because this study is concerned only with products provided to businesses, the roster is substantially narrowed. Nonetheless, a large variety must be accounted for. The discussion can proceed on two levels. A definition can be developed from surveys of where business firms bank; or it can be determined by a deductive process about business needs for banking services and knowledge about how banks make decisions on which customers to seek as clients. The literature contains examples of both of these procedures.

Studies that relied on survey data were largely motivated by the requirements of bank merger litigation or regulatory agency decisions on new charters and branch or merger applications. The deductive procedure was generally utilized by empirical studies of bank structure and will be followed in this study. The findings of the survey literature will be cited, however, to corroborate the assertions made about the appropriate market definition.

The core services of the bank-customer relationship are the loan and deposit functions. Except for the payroll and possibly petty cash requirements of remote plants and offices, businesses hold their deposits in the banks from which they borrow. Thus, the lending arrangement is the major decision variable of the business-bank relationship.

Bank costs in assessing information about a firm's activities to monitor credit needs, probability of losses, and deposit potential is a crucial variable in determining the expected profitability of the customer. Costs incurred by businesses in developing and transmitting the required information is a crucial variable for businesses in determining the choice of bank. The size of these costs for both the bank and the business is a function of the distance between the customer and the bank and the reliability of the financial data regularly developed by the business.

Small businesses do not systematically produce the financial data required by bank loan officers. Decisions to lend to these firms require substantial interaction between the banker and the businessman. Loans to small businesses, therefore, entail substantial communication costs as the distance between the bank and the business increases. Since small businesses require a small number of loan dollars, cost per dollar of loan rises rapidly with increased distance. Although other bank services to small businesses may not all have these stringent locational economies, the central position of the loaning function in choosing a bank connection implies that the relevant market for small businesses is, in general, highly localized.

This discussion suggests that the geographic size of bank markets for services rendered to a business is a function of the size of the business. Small businesses are strongly confined to the locality in which they are domiciled, medium-sized businesses can search somewhat more broadly, and large businesses are not constrained by geography in choosing their bank.[1] One qualifica-

---

[1] This description of the confines of banking markets, which is probably the most widely accepted view, was first proposed and utilized by David A. Alhadeff, *Monopoly and Competition in Banking*, Berkeley, California, 1954.

tion on bank size is required for this definition. The legal restriction on the size of loan relative to bank capital as well as managerial prudence implies that large businesses cannot be served by small banks except as a secondary source.

This description of a bank market certainly describes reality for large firms. These concerns, no matter where they are domiciled in the country, are visited regularly by representatives of many banks and can and do deal with banks at great distances. The highly localized nature of bank markets for small businesses has been extensively documented by empirical studies of individual bank markets.[2] The major uncertainty with this deductive description of bank markets is the ability of so-called medium-sized firms to bank outside of their immediate locality. The discussion suggests that, in large part, this depends upon the state of the firm's financial planning, but little information is available upon which to make informed judgments. Empirical studies suggest that bank markets are highly localized until the business reaches a substantial asset size; but such studies have been conducted for only a few cities and may not be representative.

Although the description of banking markets given above is appealing on logical grounds, it is not operational for statistical testing. There is no way to move from the term "highly localized" to a general geographic description, such as central business district, city, county, standard metropolitan statistical area (SMSA), or state. It has even been argued, with some convincing logic, that the geographic delineation of bank markets depends upon the degree of branching restriction.[3] Banks with branches tend to standardize their prices and procedures for handling customer services throughout their system. Markets dominated by unit banks tend to be more fragmented since bank policies vary between individual managements. If this line of reasoning is accepted, there is no unique or correct general geographic de-

---

[2] For some examples, see George G. Kaufman, *Business Firms and Households View Commercial Banks: A Survey of Appleton, Wisconsin,* Chicago, 1967, and *Customers View Bank Markets and Services: A Survey of Elkhart, Indiana,* Chicago, 1967; Lynn A. Styles, *Businesses View Banking Services: A Survey of Cedar Rapids, Iowa,* Chicago, 1967.

[3] Bernard Shull and Paul M. Horvitz, "Branch Banking and the Structure of Competition," *National Banking Review,* Washington, D. C., March 1964.

scription of banking markets. Each market must be studied separately and its boundaries identified empirically. Such a procedure is, of course, not feasible for a study that attempts to develop a general measure of the performance of bank markets; both because of the large amount of resources required to delineate banking markets and because custom-made market delineations are subject to endless questions of how changes in the definition of particular markets would alter the results.

In this study, banking markets are defined to be coterminus with SMSA's. This definition was chosen because of the availability of data to represent variations in the demand for banking services between standard metropolitan statistical areas. In light of the discussion above, it is clear that this definition introduces some specification error into the estimates. There is reason to believe, however, that these errors will not overwhelm the price-structure relationship, if one exists.

SMSA's are defined to include a geographic area which has some homogeneity at least in the sense of being a cohesive market area. This assumes that transportation between various points within an SMSA can be efficiently accomodated. Although the empirical studies of local bank markets suggests that, at least in unit bank areas, the SMSA definition is too broad, there is little doubt that banks included in this study can, if they desire, deal with businesses of even the smallest size in any part of their SMSA. All that is required to defend this market description for the purpose at hand is that adjacent banks in an SMSA feel the pressure of competition from one anothers presence and that their pricing policies are impacted by the proximity of other banks.

The following section presents the parameter estimates and statistical tests on models 3 and 4, described in Chapter 2. It should be remembered that these models are derived from equation 1. But, equation 2 implied that a profit maximizing bank would accept or reject customers based on a decision rule that took account of the expected profitability of the customer through a planning horizon covering the customers expected purchases over at least several years. Moreover, because of the form of the data available from the bank customer profiles, the characteristics captured in the regressions on models 3 and 4 are a conglomeration of variables that describe elements of the customer-bank relationship with mixed time periods: the mean deposit balance covers the twelve months preceeding the survey; length of relationship covers the full length of time the customer has dealt with the bank; time in debt covers the twelve preceeding months; interest rate is the rate after the last change in the prime rate; loan size is the amount of loans outstanding at the time the survey was taken (see Appendixes A and B for the form and description of the data utilized). Thus, because of misspecified time elements, specification errors are introduced into the regressions that will be presented.

Even if data could be collected to describe the customer relationship through time, errors would exist because the model implies that the bank sets its prices to make a profit, given the customer's expected use of bank resources and the deposit balances that will be supplied. There are bound to be differences between expectations and the actual results.

Errors are also introduced by the form of the variables. A number of questions in the survey requested subjective answers to questions scaled into two, three, or four partitions. Information on these aspects of the customer relationship was thought to be valuable and there was no way to get at them directly.

The statistical problems enumerated above are worth noting, but with all of these shortcomings the data from the bank customer profiles are vastly superior to the data available to all prior empirical studies of the relationship between bank market structures and prices for business services. Moreover, largely because of better data, the models estimated are substantially more realistic than those utilized in prior studies.

PARAMETER ESTIMATES AND STATISTICAL TESTS OF MODEL 3

Model 3 was formulated to estimate the impact of market

TABLE 2. Regressions on Model 3, All Customers in SMSA's, Interest Rate Dependent

	All Customers (1)		No Collateral (2)		Collateralized 100 Per Cent or More (3)
Interest rate (mean)	6.416		6.359		6.706
1. Log original amount	−0.1802	(1)	−0.2312	(4)	−0.1362
	2.5219		2.4768		2.6168
	17.34[a]		18.72[a]		4.96[a]
	0.20		0.28		0.12
2. Limited branch dummy	−0.3610	(2)	−0.3651	(1)	−0.6454
	0.55		0.60		0.44
	15.33[a]		13.57[a]		9.17[a]
	0.17		0.21		0.22
3. Population increase	0.0151	(3)	0.0107	(2)	0.0 198
	7.47		8.10		6.95
	14.84[a]		8.89[a]		6.70[a]
	0.17		0.54		0.16
4. Log total deposits (SMSA)	0.1858	(4)	0.1452	(3)	0.2385
	1.9879		2.0649		1.9435
	11.83[a]		7.92[a]		5.89[a]
	0.13		.12		0.14
5. Concentration	0.5275	(5)	0.3604	(8)	0.5182
	0.68		0.66		0.69
	10.03[a]		5.89[a]		3.57[a]
	0.11		0.09		0.09
6. Mean deposit	−0.2672	(9)	−0.2303	(10)	−0.3921
	.0408		0.0464		0.0275
	5.39[a]		3.52[a]		2.22[b]
	0.06		0.06		0.05
7. Log bank size	−0.1032	(7)	−0.0865	(6)	−0.1904
	2.0979		2.1476		2.0450
	5.37[a]		3.70[a]		3.79[a]
	0.06		0.06		0.09
8. Deposit fluctuation	0.0407	(10)	0.0267	(7)	0.0787
	1.70		1.72		1.67
	4.98[a]		2.73[a]		3.59[a]
	0.06		0.04		0.09
9. Length of lending arrangement	−0.0487	(13)	−0.0141	(13)	−0.0387
	2.66		2.69		2.60
	4.25[a]		1.04		1.31
	0.05		0.02		0.03
10. Time in debt	0.0081	(12)	0.0029	(14)	0.0037
	10.03		9.71		10.63
	3.60[a]		1.17		0.54
	0.04		0.02		0.01

structure variables on loan rates to business customers. Table 2 contains three regressions. The first, column 1, utilizes the profiles of all customers in banks domiciled in SMSA's. The second, column 2, is on the subset of customers who provide

TABLE 2—(*Concluded*)

	All Customers (1)		No Collateral (2)		Collateralized 100 Per Cent or More (3)
11. Unit bank dummy	−0.0843	(6)	−0.1451	(5)	−0.3166
	0.34		0.28		0.48
	3.27ᵃ		4.77ᵃ		4.31ᵃ
	0.04		0.08		0.10
12. Other bank	−0.0468	(14)	−0.0134	(12)	−0.0773
	0.26		0.26		0.26
	2.83ᵃ		0.68		1.80
	0.03		0.01		0.04
13. Account activity	−0.0208	(8)	−0.0304	(11)	0.0435
	1.84		1.90		1.69
	2.81ᵃ		3.58ᵃ		2.14
	0.03		0.06		0.05
14. Other services	−0.368	(11)	−0.0280	(9)	−0.1396
	0.23		0.22		0.25
	2.27ᵇ		1.45		3.35ᵃ
	0.03		0.02		0.08
Intercept	6.525		6.791		6.706
R^2	0.18		0.25		0.18
F	122.97ᵃ		93.90ᵃ		26.09ᵃ
N	7614		4000		1729

NOTE: The scalings for variables in all regressions on model 3 are: interest rates, in per cent; average deposits, hundreds of dollars; log original amount, $Log_{10}X$, where X = hundreds of dollars; log bank size, $Log_{10}X$, where X = hundreds of dollars; log total deposits of SMSA, $Log_{10}X$, where X = thousands of dollars; log business assets, $Log_{10}X$ where X = hundreds of dollars.

Within each column for each variable, the first number is the regression coefficient; the second, the mean; the third, the T value; and the fourth, the partial correlation coefficient.

In column 1, the variables are listed in descending order of the size of their net relationship to the dependent variable, as measured by the partial correlation coefficient. The numbers in parentheses in columns 2 and 3 indicate the order of variables if listed by the partial correlation coefficient.

ᵃ Significant at the .01 level.
ᵇ Significant at the .05 level.

no collateral to the bank. The third, column 3, is on customers whose loans are collateralized 100 per cent or more.

Regressions on these three sets of customers will be presented for most of the tests in this study. The "all customer" regressions are shown because they include all the available customer profiles; the data on partially collateralized customers would otherwise not be utilized. In addition, this form is more comparable than the other two to prior research which attempted to measure the price-structure relationship.

The regression on uncollateralized customers is presented because of the belief that these customers most nearly fit the implications of the bank pricing model specified in equations 1 and 2. The collateralized customer regressions are presented because of the belief that these customers are treated in a distinctly different manner from those with no collateral. Handling collateral is an additional cost of the banking relationship. But, the collateral greatly reduces the risk exposure of the bank. More important, there is a high probability that the uncollateralized customer has a long-run profitable relationship with the bank; whereas, the collateralized customer has a high probability of having an intermittent relationship or of being a new customer. Thus, regressions on collateralized customers provide insights into the costs and risks associated with business lending. Differences in parameter estimates between noncollateralized and collateralized loan customers provide insights into differences between long- and short-term relationship customers.

As can be seen, the R^2 in all three regressions are relatively low; but they are all statistically significant at the 1 per cent level, which indicates a high statistical probability that the independent variables have an influence on loan rates.

In the regression on all customers, column 1, the variables are listed in descending order of the size of their net relationship to the dependent variable, as measured by the partial correlation coefficient. The coefficient of all but one of the independent variables is statistically significant at the 1 per cent level and that one is statistically significant at the 5 per cent level. The five structural and market characteristic variables are among the first seven, ordered by highest net relationship to the dependent variable. All of the coefficients of the customer characteristic variables, however, have the signs implied in equation 1.

The log of the original amount of the loan has the highest net relationship to the interest rate. The original loan outstanding is a proxy for both the cost of making and administering the loan and for default risk. A substantial part of the administrative and processing costs associated with the lending function are fixed; therefore, cost per dollar of loan declines as loan size increases. The probability of default has been found to be inversely related to the size of business, and the size of loan is positively associated with business size.[4] Thus, for both variables for which size of loan is a proxy a negative sign is expected.

The log of loan size is used because of the belief that this form, more closely than absolute values, approximates the true relationship between cost and size of loan, and risk and size of loan. To test this presumption a regression was computed using absolute loan size values. As expected, both the partial relationship between the loan size and interest rate and the R^2 for the entire equation was larger when the log form was used.

Population increase, the proxy for demand for banking services, has the third highest net relationship to the interest rate on loans. Since markets with higher loan demand, other things being equal, are expected to have higher loan prices, the positive sign conforms to expectations.

The log of total bank deposits in the SMSA, which has the fourth highest net relationship with the dependent variable, is included in the model because of the findings of loan rate surveys that larger bank markets exhibit lower loan prices than do smaller markets. Again, the log rather than absolute values

[4] Geoffrey H. Moore, Thomas R. Atkinson, and Edward I. Kilberg, "Risk and Returns in Small Business Financing," *Financing Small Business*, Part 1, Federal Reserve System, Washington, D.C., April 1958, p. 44.

is used after testing for goodness of fit between these two forms. The positive sign of this variable is contrary to expectations from loan rate surveys. But this is a net relationship, after taking account of bank size, demand characteristics, market structure, size of loan, and customer characteristics. This suggests that the observed simple relationship between market size and loan rates confounds the effects of other variables that are not included. But, it should also be noted that a positive net relationship between market size and loan rates has a higher probability of occurrence during periods of relatively tight monetary conditions, such as have prevailed since mid-1966 to the date of the customer survey, than during other phases of the cycle. The relatively low ceiling rates of Regulation Q, during such periods, impose a heavy cost of funds burden on the larger banks, which place a relatively heavy reliance on purchased money. The positive relationship between size of bank and size of market suggests that the positive sign of the size of market coefficient might then be caused, in part, by the larger banks passing on the relative rise in their cost of funds.

Deposits are valuable to the bank; hence, the negative sign of the deposit balance coefficient is expected.

A bank size variable is included because of the often reported negative relationship between bank size and loan rates. The log rather than the absolute size is used because of the belief that any size effect would not be linear but rather would be large at small sizes and grow with progressively smaller increments as bank size increases.

In the studies that show a negative relationship between bank size and loan rate, other crucial variables are not accounted for. Large banks generally deal with a greater proportion of large customers than do smaller banks. Since loan size is a proxy for risk and cost, this difference could explain the bank size effect that is usually observed. But, size of loan is explicitly included in this regression.

The bank size variable could reflect economies of scale. But recent empirical studies indicate that when $40 million in asset size is reached, relatively few additional economies remain as bank size increases.[5] Or, another possibility, which will be explored more fully in the discussion of the regressions on deposit balances, is that the profit strategy of different sized banks places a systematically different stress on the loan and deposit prices of the customer relationship. Whatever the cause, the coefficient of this variable is statistically significant and has a negative sign, which conforms to prior results reported on the simple relationship.

A fluctuating deposit is less desirable than a stable deposit; hence, the positive sign is expected. The bank's knowledge of its customers' needs increases and its risk exposure in the relationship decreases with an increasing length of lending arrangement; thus, the negative sign is expected. Increased time in debt raises the amount of bank funds committed to the customer with other revenues and deposits taken into account; the positive sign is expected. Businesses that deal with multiple banks are expected to have a competitive edge in bargaining on rates. The negative sign is also expected because it is good strategy for businesses that deal with more than one bank to bargain for the minimum loan rate and produce the required profitability in the relationship with each bank by maintaining the necessary deposit balances: Loan rates are highly visible or easily discovered by other banks whereas size of deposit balances at other banks are not known. The negative sign on account activity is a reflection of the fact that banks analyze activity and levy a charge in terms of deposit balances and, occasionally, fees for this service. Since the charge includes a profit element, high activity customers add to profit through balances and this is reflected in loan rate reductions. Customers that purchase "other services" are expected to provide additional profits to the bank; hence, the negative relationship with loan rates conforms to expectations.

The differences in the regressions on uncollateralized and

[5] See Fredrick W. Bell and Neil B. Murphy, *Returns to Scale in Commercial Banking*, Research Report, Federal Reserve Bank of Boston.

fully collateralized customers contain a number of interesting insights. First, the variation in the ordering of variables with respect to net relationship with loan rates is instructive. For uncollateralized customers, the loan size variable has the highest net relationship. For collateralized customers, it ranks fourth, below the demand proxy, one of the branch restriction variables, and below market size. This difference is expected because loan size is virtually independent of risk for fully collateralized customers but risk is an important element in setting the loan rate for noncollateralized customers. The much higher negative coefficient on the loan size variable for uncollateralized customers shows again that risk on fully collateralized customers' loans does not decline as loan size increases. The switch in sign of the coefficient of "account activity" between these regressions is explained by the differences in the bank-customer relationship. Fully collateralized customers are less likely to be long-term profitable customers than are uncollateralized customers; hence, the profitability of account activity of the former are less likely to be offset in other parts of the relationship.

Turning now to the structure variables, the concentration variable is the proportion of total deposits in the SMSA controlled by the offices of the three largest holders of deposits in that particular SMSA. The deposit data were collected on an office basis because of the problem of computing market concentration ratios in states that allow statewide branching. In such states, the largest bank in a market may be the branches of a system with its home office in another SMSA. The signs of the coefficients of the concentration variables are positive in all three regressions. This implies that loan rates rise as the proportion of total deposits in the market held by the three largest banks increase.

Branch restrictions are partitioned into three classes: markets in unit bank states, markets in restricted branching states, and markets in states that permit statewide branching. Thus, there are three branching restriction variables. In each variable, markets which are in the class are coded one; the other markets are coded zero. Two branching restriction variables are shown in the regressions. The third, statewide branching, is impounded in the intercept.

As can be seen, the limited branching dummy variable has the second highest net relationship to interest rate. More important, it is statistically significant at the 1 per cent level in all three regressions and has a negative sign in all three regressions. The unit bank dummy variable has a smaller net relationship to interest rates. But, it is statistically significant at the 1 per cent level and has a negative sign in all three regressions. The coefficient of the limited branching dummy is larger than the coefficient of the unit banking in all three corresponding regressions. These results imply interest rates are lowest in limited branching markets, highest in statewide branching markets, and that rates in unit banking markets are between these two.

The popular belief that business size is an important determinant of the loan rate accorded bank customers suggests that this variable should be explicitly included in the model. Table 3 contains the parameter estimates of model 3 with the log of business assets included as an independent variable. The log form is used because it is believed that the incremental impact on loan price declines as size of business increases. Since almost 40 per cent of the customer profiles did not include business size data, regressions which include business assets have a substantially smaller number of observations than those in Table 2.

All three regressions shown in Table 3 are statistically significant; moreover, the R^2's are marginally higher than in Table 2 in all three corresponding equations. This suggests that business size influences the interest price decision. It is also interesting to note that the mean interest rates are virtually identical on corresponding regressions in Tables 2 and 3, which suggests that the availability of financial data in bank files is not a function of the interest charged.

TABLE 3.   Regressions on Model 3, Customers With Asset Data, Interest Rate Dependent

	All Customers (1)		No Collateral (2)		Collateralized 100 Per Cent or More (3)
Interest rate (mean)	6.407		6.343		6.613
1. Limited branch dummy	−0.3665	(1)	−0.3573	(1)	−0.6215
	0.56		0.60		0.40
	12.49ᵃ		11.01ᵃ		6.69ᵃ
	0.17		0.21		0.21
2. Log business assets	−0.1582	(2)	−0.1288	(9)	−0.1045
	3.7041		3.7606		3.5920
	10.88ᵃ		7.89ᵃ		2.07ᵇ
	0.15		0.15		0.07
3. Population increase	0.0129	(5)	0.0080	(3)	0.0184
	7.19		7.71		6.50
	9.74ᵃ		5.16ᵃ		4.46ᵃ
	0.14		0.10		0.14
4. Log total deposits (SMSA)	0.1624	(4)	0.1269	(2)	0.2702
	1.9987		2.0830		1.9168
	8.51ᵃ		6.00ᵃ		4.57ᵃ
	0.12		0.11		0.15
5. Concentration	0.4585	(6)	0.3231	(7)	0.4798
	0.67		0.66		0.69
	7.17ᵃ		4.45ᵃ		2.29ᵇ
	0.10		0.08		0.07
6. Deposit fluctuation	0.0429	(10)	0.0348	(8)	0.0632
	1.76		1.77		1.79
	4.40ᵃ		3.08ᵃ		2.18ᵇ
	0.06		0.06		0.07
7. Length of lending arrangement	−0.0527	(15)	−0.0062	(6)	−0.0969
	2.70		2.72		2.66
	3.70ᵃ		0.38		2.39ᵇ
	0.05		0.01		0.08
8. Unit bank dummy	−0.1151	(7)	−0.1460	(4)	−0.3465
	0.35		0.29		0.52
	3.62ᵃ		4.03ᵃ		3.60ᵃ
	0.05		0.08		0.11
9. Log original amount	−0.0498	(3)	−0.1308	(11)	−0.1047
	2.6319		2.5805		2.7805
	2.89ᵃ		6.47ᵃ		2.05ᵇ
	0.04		0.12		0.06
10. Mean deposit	−0.1522	(11)	−0.1495	(15)	−0.2714
	0.0473		0.0505		0.0351
	2.82ᵃ		1.92		1.43
	0.04		0.04		0.05

TABLE 3—(*Concluded*)

	All Customers (1)		No Collateral (2)		Collateralized 100 Per Cent or More (3)
11. Account activity	−0.0215	(9)	−0.0336	(10)	0.0534
	1.93		1.97		1.82
	2.51b		3.49		2.06b
	0.04		0.07		0.07
12. Time in debt	0.0065	(14)	0.0020	(14)	0.0138
	9.99		9.63		10.73
	2.34b		0.67		1.47
	0.03		0.01		0.05
13. Log bank size	−0.0559	(12)	−0.0485	(13)	−0.1045
	2.1075		2.1486		3.5920
	2.28b		1.72		2.07b
	0.03		0.03		0.07
14. Other services	−0.0344	(13)	−0.0338	(5)	−0.1561
	0.25		0.24		0.28
	1.83		1.55		2.91a
	0.03		0.03		0.09
15. Other bank	0.0240	(8)	0.0860	(12)	−0.1022
	0.29		0.28		0.29
	1.16		3.52a		1.78
	0.02		0.07		0.06
Intercept	6.813		6.983		6.977
R^2	0.19		0.25		0.19
F	77.40a		60.63a		15.44a
N	4957		2707		984

NOTE: See the notes to Table 2.

a Significant at the .01 level.

b Significant at the .05 level.

As can be seen, the inclusion of the log of business assets affected the three regressions in Table 3 differently. For non-collateralized customers, asset size has the second highest net relationship with interest rates but loan size still has a relatively high relationship, ranked third, and is statistically significant at the 1 per cent level. On the other hand, business size is ranked ninth and is only significant at the 5 per cent level for collateralized customers while loan size is ranked eleventh and is also significant at the 5 per cent level. This finding conforms to expectations. It is reasonable that business size should not be important when the loan is fully collateralized. In the noncollateralized regression the strong relationship between loan size and interest rate and between business size and loan rate implies that business size has an influence on loan rates independent of loan size.

The change in statistical significance of the bank size coefficient should also be noted. It is not significant in the noncollateralized customers regressions. This suggests that the significant relationship in Table 2 and in many other statistical studies may be largely due to the relationship between bank size and business size. However, the signs of the coefficients are still all negative, but all are smaller than in Table 2.

The size and signs of the coefficients of the structural variables are most interesting. The coefficients of concentration are positive in all three equations but in the fully collateralized regression it is only statistically significant at the 5 per cent level. Moreover, the size of the coefficients are somewhat smaller than Table 2. The branch restriction coefficients are all negative and statistically significant at the 1 per cent level. Thus, the indicated relationship is the same as in Table 2 with approximately the same size coefficients in corresponding regressions.

To properly evaluate the findings of the estimates presented above, it is desirable, at this point, to review the empirical literature on the question of the relationship of bank prices to the structure of bank markets. The major studies in this area have invariably used loan rate as the dependent variable. But the models included only loan size and loan maturity to depict customer relationship variables. A major controversy in this literature is over the question of whether the demand for banking services is properly specified by some demographic surrogate or whether it is necessary to explicitly include region to properly depict demand variations between markets. Thus, Edwards[6] used data from the 1955 Federal Reserve Business Loan Survey to estimate the parameters of the following re-

---

[6] Franklin R. Edwards, *Concentration and Competition in Commercial Banking: A Statistical Study,* Federal Reserve Bank of Boston, 1964, p. 64.

gression: Interest rates on business loans $= f$ (concentration, percentage change in manufacturing employment, average loan size, percentage of loans with maturities under one year). He reported that concentration had a statistically significant positive coefficient. Flechsig[7] utilized identical data to estimate the parameters of: Interest rates on business loans $= f$ (concentration, average loan size, percentage change in employment, region). He found the concentration coefficient was not statistically significant.[8]

Although neither of the two studies discussed above found the coefficient of a branch restriction variable, when it was included in the model, to be statistically significant, the regional concentration of the three types of branching restriction argues for the inclusion of a regional variable in the model. Table 4 contains the parameter estimates when a six partition regional variable is included in model 3.[9] As can be seen, all three equations are statistically significant at the 1 per cent level. Moreover, the inclusion of the regional variable very substantially raises the R^2's compared to those in Tables 2 and 3.

The evidence from these regressions strongly suggests that the regional effect on loan rates is very significant and should be included in the specification of demand variation between markets. Region 6, which includes the Pacific Coast states to the Rocky Mountains, has the second highest net relationship to interest rates. The coefficients of Regions 5 and 4 are also statistically significant at the 1 per cent level in all three regressions; whereas Region 2 is mixed, with two regressions

[7] Theodore G. Flechsig, *Banking Market Structure and Performance in Metropolitan Areas*, Board of Governors of the Federal Reserve System, 1965.

[8] The Edwards and Flechsig studies are cited to note the problem of the regional impact on loan rates and to show the models that have been used. Both studies also suffer from other problems largely due to the data available to them from the Federal Reserve Loan Surveys. For a critique of these studies and an analysis of data deficiencies see Almarin Phillips, "Evidence on Concentration in Banking Markets and Interest Rates," *Federal Reserve Bulletin*, June 1967, pp. 916–926.

[9] To maintain as much comparability as possible with prior research, the regional partitions are identical to those used by Flechsig. Flechsig's map of the regional partitions, *op cit.*, p. 74, is reproduced as Appendix C.

TABLE 4. Regressions on Model 3, All Customers in SMSA's, With a Six Partition Regional Variable, Interest Rate Dependent

	All Customers (1)		No Collateral (2)		Collateralized 100 Per Cent or More (3)
Interest rate (mean)	6.416		6.359		6.558
1. Log original amount	−0.1931	(1)	−0.2494	(3)	−0.1319
	2.5219		2.4768		2.6168
	18.80[a]		20.94[a]		4.75[a]
	0.21		0.32		0.11
2. Region 6	0.7610	(2)	0.8398	(12)	0.5583
	0.07		0.07		0.07
	17.86[a]		19.17[a]		2.35[b]
	.20		0.29		0.06
3. Population increase	0.0139	(3)	0.0094	(1)	0.0209
	7.47		8.10		6.95
	13.49[a]		7.88[a]		6.75[a]
	0.15		0.12		0.16
4. Log total deposits (SMSA)	0.1571	(4)	0.1112	(2)	0.2286
	1.9879		2.0649		1.9435
	9.88[a]		6.23[a]		5.46[a]
	0.11		0.10		0.13
5. Concentration	0.4622	(5)	0.3276	(9)	0.4465
	0.68		0.66		0.69
	8.79[a]		5.46[a]		2.93[a]
	0.10		0.09		0.07
6. Region 5	0.2386	(9)	0.1487	(6)	0.3094
	0.12		0.08		0.17
	7.66[a]		3.67[a]		3.60[a]
	0.09		0.06		0.09
7. Region 4	0.1679	(10)	0.0971	(5)	0.3200
	0.23		0.21		0.31
	5.68[a]		2.75[a]		3.75[a]
	0.07		0.04		0.09
8. Log bank size	−0.1003	(15)	−0.0321	(4)	−0.1939
	2.0979		2.1476		2.0450
	5.30[a]		1.41		3.83[a]
	0.06		0.02		0.09
9. Mean deposit	−0.2493	(8)	−0.2492	(11)	−0.4155
	0.0408		0.0464		0.0275
	5.15[a]		3.99[a]		2.36[b]
	0.06		0.06		0.06
10. Unit bank dummy	0.2038	(6)	0.2479	(18)	−0.1077
	0.34		0.28		0.4829
	4.73[a]		5.05[a]		0.45
	0.05		0.08		0.01

TABLE 4—(*Concluded*)

	All Customers (1)		No Collateral (2)		Collateralized 100 Per Cent or More (3)
11. Deposit fluctuation	0.0323	(11)	0.0253	(8)	0.0675
	1.70		1.72		1.67
	4.03ª		2.71ª		3.07ª
	0.05		0.04		0.07
12. Length of lending arrangement	−0.0401	(16)	−0.0156	(16)	0.0317
	2.66		2.69		2.60
	3.58ª		1.20		1.08
	0.04		0.02		0.03
13. Region 2	0.0683	(7)	0.1162	(13)	0.1211
	0.15		0.14		0.12
	3.17ª		4.81ª		1.83
	0.04		0.08		0.04
14. Other services	−0.0470	(14)	−0.0269	(7)	−0.1455
	0.23		0.22		0.25
	2.96ª		1.45		3.48ª
	0.03		0.02		0.08
15. Other bank	−0.0432	(19)	0.0015	(14)	−0.0775
	0.26		0.26		0.26
	2.67ª		0.08		1.81
	0.03		0.01		0.04
16. Time in debt	0.0055	(18)	0.0014	(19)	0.0027
	10.03		9.71		10.63
	2.50ᵇ		0.58		0.39
	0.03		0.01		0.01
17. Limited branch dummy	0.0618	(13)	0.0838	(17)	−0.2159
	0.55		0.60		0.44
	1.77		2.27ᵇ		0.94
	0.02		0.04		0.02
18. Region 3	0.0359	(17)	0.0241	(15)	0.0939
	0.16		0.15		0.16
	1.63		0.96		1.41
	0.02		0.02		0.03
19. Account activity	−0.0088	(12)	−0.0196	(10)	0.0536
	1.84		1.90		1.69
	1.21		2.40ᵇ		2.62ª
	0.01		0.04		0.06
Intercept	6.191		6.328		6.248
R^2	.23		0.32		0.19
F	116.04ª		98.43ª		20.62ª
N	7614		4000		1729

NOTE: See the notes to Table 2.

[a] Significant at the .01 level.

[b] Significant at the .05 level.

significant and the third not. The coefficients of Region 3 are
not statistically significant in any of the regressions. Region 1
is embedded in the intercept; thus, its significance cannot be
directly tested. Region 1 contains the tier of states in the north-
eastern part of the United States which traditionally have the
lowest interest rates. Thus, the positive signs of the other five
regions indicate the positive rate differential between each of
the regions and the Northeast.

All three concentration coefficients have a positive sign and
are statistically significant at the 1 per cent level. Moreover,
concentration has a higher net relationship with interest rates
than does either of the two branch restriction variables, in all
three regressions.

The unit banking dummy is statistically significant at the
1 per cent level in the all customer and noncollateralized customer regression, but the coefficient of the fully collateralized
regression is not significant even at the 5 per cent level. It is
important to note that the coefficients that are statistically significant have a positive sign.

The limited branching coefficient is significant at the 5 per
cent level in the noncollateralized regression and not statistically significant in the other two regressions. But the coefficient
that is significant has a positive sign.

These findings imply statewide branching markets have lower
loan rates than either restricted branching markets or unit
banking markets. Moreover, the size of the coefficient suggests
that restricted branching markets have lower rates than unit
banking markets. But the evidence on restricted markets is
substantially weaker than the estimates provided in Tables 2
and 3. There is some reason to argue that there is no difference
in loan price between restricted branching and statewide branching markets. This is implied by the lack of statistical significance
of the restricted branching coefficient in the all customer and
fully collateralized customer regressions.

The theoretical arguments used to justify the choice of SMSA
definitions as the appropriate delineation of banking markets

implied that the market power of banks and, therefore, their ability to influence price is functionally related to the size of business. Moreover, the regressions in Table 3 indicated that business size influenced rates charged. It is, therefore, desirable to estimate the influence of market structure on different sized businesses with the regional variables included in the equation.

Regressions were, therefore, computed on customers for whom business asset data were available, partitioned into three size classes; up to one-half million dollars, more than one-half million to one million, and more than one million to five million. These regressions, computed separately for all customers, noncollateralized customers, and fully collateralized customers are shown in Appendix D. It should be remembered that there was some question both about the size of firms that should be included in the "medium size" category and whether this size business is affected by market power. The parameters of the two largest classes are, therefore, of particular interest. In the collateralized 100 per cent or more category the regressions for the two larger business size classes could not be computed because all of the observations for statewide branching markets were in Region 6; see Appendix E for distributions of customer by region branching restriction and business size.

The F tests indicate that all seven regressions shown in Appendix D are statistically significant at the 1 per cent probability level. In both sets of three regressions mean loan rates decline, as expected, with increased business size. Interestingly, the coefficient of Region 6 is positive, statistically significant and has the highest net relationship with the dependent variable in five of the six regressions on all customers and noncollateralized customers.

Parameter estimates and test statistics of the structural variables are summarized in Table 5. As can be seen, the coefficients of all of the regressions in both the unit branching and restricted branching categories have positive signs. But, only two coefficients are significant at the 1 per cent level and one at the 5 per cent level. Of great interest is the fact that all three of the significant coefficients are in the smallest business size class. None of the coefficients in either of the two larger business size classes is statistically significant.

The parameter estimates and test statistics for the concentration variable are shown in the bottom third of Table 5. As can be seen, in all seven regressions the coefficients of the concentration variable are positive and all are statistically significant, four at the 1 per cent level and three at the 5 per cent level. Moreover, the regression coefficients in the three size classes, for the two types of customers, are close in absolute size.

TABLE 5. Parameter Estimates and Test Statistics for Structural Variables, Customers With Asset Data, Three Size Classes, Interest Rate Dependent

	Asset Size (millions of dollars)					
	$0 \leq .5$		$.5 \leq 1$		$1 \leq 5$	
Unit banking						
All customers	(5)	.3397	(13)	.0987	(14)	.1236
		.34		.35		.36
		4.80[a]		.67		1.03
		.09		.03		.04
Noncollateralized	(4)	.3423	(11)	.2407	(17)	.0481
		.25		.28		.30
		4.36[a]		1.70		.38
		.11		.09		.02
Collateralized 100 per cent	(11)	.5574				
or more		.52				
		1.22		c		c
		.05				
Restricted branching						
All customers	(13)	.1285	(19)	.0020	(12)	.1680
		.56		.55		.55
		2.23[b]		.02		1.58
		.04		.01		.06
Noncollateralized	(11)	.0948	(14)	.0976	(16)	.0910
		.62		.61		.59
		1.62		.84		.89
		.04		.05		.04
Collateralized 100 per cent	(17)	.3478				
or more		.41				
		.79		c		c
		.03				

In conclusion, the estimates from the regressions on the three size classes of business customers imply that loan rates are positively related to the level of concentration of deposits in the bank market and that size of firm, at least up to $5 million in assets, does not influence this relationship. The evidence on the relationship between loan rates and branching restrictions suggests that a positive relationship exists for firms up to a half million dollars in assets. The evidence is strong that for such smaller sized firms unit banking markets have higher loan rates than do restricted branching and statewide banking markets. The data also suggest that loan rates for small firms are higher in restricted than in statewide branching markets. But, the evidence is weaker on this latter relationship. The

TABLE 5—(*Concluded*)

	Asset Size (*millions of dollars*)					
	| 0 ≤ .5		| .5 ≤ 1		| 1 ≤ 5	
Concentration						
All customers	(3)	.4813	(4)	.4107	(8)	.4752
		.67		.68		.67
		5.62[a]		2.27[b]		3.37[a]
		.10		.09		.12
Noncollateralized	(7)	.3228	(6)	.4046	(5)	.4503
		.66		.67		.66
		3.17[a]		2.10[b]		2.93[a]
		.08		.11		.14
Collateralized 100 per cent	(4)	.6835				
or more		.70				
		2.40[b]		[c]		[c]
		.10				

NOTE: Within each column for each variable, the first number is the regression coefficient; the second, the mean; the third, the T value; and the fourth, the partial correlation coefficient. The numbers in parentheses indicate the order of the variables within their respective regressions.

SOURCE: Appendix D.

[a] Significant at the .01 level.

[b] Significant at the .05 level.

[c] These regressions could not be computed because of the sample of customers.

evidence is strong that loan rates to firms with more than one-half million dollars in assets are not affected by branching restriction.

PARAMETER ESTIMATES AND STATISTICAL TESTS OF
MODEL 4

The discussion in Chapter 2 argued that businesses compensate banks through a vector of prices: with interest payments when loans are outstanding, by maintaining deposit balances throughout the period of the relationship, and on occasion with cash fees. Although interest is probably the dominant payment businesses make to banks, in terms of the total value of payments received by banks, the deposit component of the price vector is also an important part of total compensation. From the business viewpoint, the cost of maintaining deposit balances is a major expenditure. This is certainly true even in explicit costs for large firms and it is true of the sum of explicit and implicit costs for the smaller firms. If deposit balances are voluntarily held by small firms they could at least purchase an expanded set of bank services for these deposits. But even smaller firms probably hold some deposit balances in excess of desired balances because of bank requirements. In this section, the parameter estimates of model 4 are presented and analyzed to determine if there is a relationship between the deposit component of the price vector for bank services and market structure.

Parameter estimates and test statistics for model 4 are shown in Table 6; the regression on all customers is shown in column 1, noncollateralized customers are shown in column 2, and fully collateralized customers, in column 3.

All three regressions are statistically significant at the 1 per cent level. Although the R^2's are not large, they are larger than the R^2's for the corresponding regressions in Table 2, with interest rate dependent.

In the all customer regression, the coefficients of eight of the thirteen variables are statistically significant; seven at the 1 per cent level and one at the 5 per cent level. The first five variables,

TABLE 6. Regressions on Model 4, All Customers in SMSA's, Average Deposits Dependent

	All Customers (1)		No Collateral (2)		Collateralized 100 Per Cent or More (3)
Average deposit (mean)	408.44		463.89		274.81
1. Original amount	0.1959	(1)	0.1959	(1)	0.1393
	1244.78		1241.44		1356.90
	32.07[a]		27.92[a]		15.12[a]
	0.35		0.40		0.34
2. Account activity	233.05	(2)	242.29	(2)	184.05
	1.84		1.90		1.69
	14.48[a]		12.80[a]		7.06[a]
	0.16		0.20		0.17
3. Other bank	234.40	(3)	244.24	(7)	83.41
	0.26		0.26		0.26
	6.54[a]		5.58[a]		1.51
	0.07		0.09		0.04
4. Interest rate	−1.32	(4)	−1.59	(6)	−0.49
	641.57		635.86		655.80
	5.27[a]		4.55[a]		1.57
	0.06		0.07		0.04
5. Time in debt	23.75	(6)	−13.06	(5)	−15.17
	10.03		9.71		10.63
	4.79[a]		2.29[b]		1.72
	0.05		0.04		0.04
6. Log bank size	127.62	(8)	89.37	(3)	130.54
	6.0979		6.1476		6.0450
	2.99[a]		1.68		1.99[b]
	0.03		0.03		0.05
7. Length of lending arrangement	68.49	(7)	69.12	(8)	44.37
	2.66		2.69		2.60
	2.70[a]		2.23[b]		1.15
	0.03		0.04		0.03
8. Other services	80.27	(5)	163.40	(12)	15.03
	0.23		0.22		0.25
	2.24[b]		3.70[a]		0.28
	0.03		0.06		0.01
9. Population increase	1.65	(9)	4.37	(11)	−2.44
	7.47		8.10		6.95
	0.72		1.58		0.62
	0.01		0.03		0.02

(Continued)

TABLE 6—(*Concluded*)

	All Customers (1)		No Collateral (2)		Collateralized 100 Per Cent or More (3)
10. Limited branch dummy	36.26	(12)	61.13	(10)	64.90
	0.55		0.60		0.44
	0.68		0.97		0.69
	0.01		0.02		0.02
11. Log total deposits (SMSA)	5.37	(10)	57.53	(14)	−0.81
	5.99		6.06		5.94
	0.15		1.37		0.02
	0.01		0.02		0.01
12. Deposit fluctuation	2.28	(11)	30.29	(13)	3.49
	1.70		1.72		1.67
	0.13		1.36		0.12
	0.01		0.02		0.01
13. Concentration	−6.74	(13)	127.33	(4)	−375.40
	0.68		0.66		0.69
	0.06		0.91		1.98[b]
	0.01		0.01		0.05
14. Unit bank dummy	0.46	(14)	39.86	(9)	72.74
	0.34		0.28		0.48
	0.01		0.57		0.75
	0.01		0.01		0.02
Intercept	−284.44		−506.98		−452.50
R^2	0.22		0.31		0.20
F	153.29[a]		125.70[a]		31.26[a]
N	7614		4000		1729

NOTE: The scalings for variables in all regressions on model 4 are: mean deposit, hundreds of dollars; log original amount, $Log_{10}X$, where X = hundreds of dollars; log bank sign, $Log_{10}X$, where X = millions of dollars; log total deposit of SMSA, $Log_{10}X$, where X = ten millions of dollars; log business assets, $Log_{10}X$, where X = hundreds of dollars; interest rate, in per cent.

Within each column for each variable, the first number is the regression coefficient; the second, the mean; the third, the T value; and the fourth, the partial correlation coefficient.

In column 1, the variables are listed in descending order of the size of their net relationship to the dependent variable, as measured by the partial correlation coefficient. The numbers in parentheses in columns 2 and 3 indicate the order of variables if listed by the partial correlation coefficient.

[a] Significant at the .01 level.
[b] Significant at the .05 level.

ordered by size of net relationship with the dependent variable, are all customer characteristics. The relatively strong relationship of the customer characteristics is very different from the relationship found in the regressions on interest rates. In those regressions, customer characteristics other than loan size rarely were among the five variables with the highest net relationship to loan rates; in terms of net relationship the demand or market characteristics were almost invariably the highest.

The regression and partial correlation coefficients for non-collateralized customers are very similar to the all-customer estimates; seven variables are statistically significant and the first seven variables ordered by size of net relationship are customer characteristics. In all three regressions, all of the coefficients of the customer characteristic variables have the expected signs.

The coefficient of only one noncustomer characteristic variable, log of bank size, is statistically significant and then only in two regressions. The positive sign on the coefficient implies that deposit balances increase with bank size after taking into account all components of the customer relationship. It should be remembered that the sign of the coefficient of this variable was invariably negative in the regressions with interest rate dependent. The positive sign in these regressions is probably explained by the fact that larger banks acquire a higher proportion of their funds in the purchased money markets and thus are subject to a greater degree of risk because of fluctuations in the cost of funds. Larger banks, therefore, value deposits more highly than smaller banks.

None of the coefficients of market size or the demand surrogate, change in population, is statistically significant. Most important, the coefficient of neither of the branch restriction dummy variables is statistically significant in any of the three equations. The coefficient of the concentration variable is not statistically significant in the first two regressions. In the fully collateralized regression it is just significant at the 5 per cent level, but it has a negative sign. We cannot explain this latter result.

48   Business Loan Costs and Bank Market Structure

TABLE 7. Regressions on Model 4, Customers With Asset Data, Average Deposits Dependent

	All Customers (1)		No Collateral (2)		Collateralized 100 Per Cent or More (3)
Average deposit (mean)	472.83		505.17		351.09
1. Original amount	0.1842	(1)	0.1742	(1)	0.1627
	1401.59		1353.47		1644.63
	20.17[a]		19.03[a]		10.12[a]
	0.28		0.34		0.31
2. Account activity	219.09	(2)	222.22	(2)	182.00
	1.93		1.97		1.82
	10.17[a]		10.12[a]		4.42[a]
	0.14		0.19		0.14
3. Log business assets	228.98	(3)	236.69	(5)	81.02
	3.7041		3.7606		3.5920
	7.25[a]		7.50[a]		1.11
	0.10		0.14		0.04
4. Time in debt	−24.63	(5)	−13.66	(9)	−11.32
	9.99		9.63		10.73
	3.62[a]		2.04[b]		0.76
	0.05		0.04		0.02
5. Interest rate	−0.94	(6)	−0.89	(6)	−0.51
	640.73		634.28		661.25
	2.61[a]		1.99[b]		0.99
	0.04		0.04		0.03
6. Log bank size	154.15	(8)	104.42	(4)	174.55
	6.1075		6.1486		6.0668
	2.48[b]		1.59		1.32
	0.04		0.03		0.04
7. Limited branch dummy	134.48	(10)	114.71	(7)	151.89
	0.56		0.60		0.40
	1.77		1.48		0.99
	0.03		0.03		0.03
8. Other services	65.53	(4)	125.11	(11)	−36.64
	0.25		0.24		0.28
	1.37		2.45[b]		0.42
	0.02		0.05		0.01
9. Length of lending arrangement	48.81	(9)	58.50	(12)	25.49
	2.70		2.72		2.66
	1.35		1.52		0.39
	0.02		0.03		0.01
10. Other bank	70.51	(15)	33.22	(13)	33.12
	0.29		0.28		0.29
	1.34		0.58		0.36
	0.02		0.01		0.01

TABLE 7—(*Concluded*)

	All Customers (1)		No Collateral (2)		Collateralized 100 Per Cent or More (3)
11. Unit bank dummy	72.71	(12)	65.74	(8)	130.16
	0.35		0.29		0.52
	0.90		0.77		0.83
	0.01		0.01		0.03
12. Deposit fluctuation	10.30	(7)	42.86	(15)	−3.03
	1.76		1.76		1.79
	0.42		1.63		0.01
13. Population increase	1.14	(11)	5.09	(10)	−3.93
	7.18		7.71		6.50
	0.34		1.40		0.59
	0.01		0.03		0.02
14. Concentration	35.92	(14)	147.34	(3)	−555.73
	0.67		0.66		0.69
	0.22		0.87		1.64
	0.00		0.17		0.05
15. Log total deposits (SMSA)	−2.06	(13)	44.13	(14)	−18.86
	5.9987		6.0830		5.9168
	0.04		0.89		0.20
	0.00		0.02		0.01
Intercept	−1453.44		−1772.92		−803.77
R^2	0.23		0.34		0.22
F	97.77[a]		92.50[a]		18.07[a]
N	4957		2707		984

NOTE: See the notes to Table 6.
[a] Significant at the .01 level.
[b] Significant at the .05 level.

The regressions on customers for which business asset data are available, with deposits the dependent variable, produced the same general results as above (see Table 7). The regressions are all statistically significant and although the R^2's are not large, they are larger than in the corresponding regressions on interest rates. Of the six variables whose coefficients are statistically significant at the 1 or 5 per cent level in both the all customer and no collateral customer regressions, five are customer characteristics; only log of bank size of the non-customer characteristic variables is statistically significant and then only in the all customer regression. None of the coefficients of change in population, size of market, or either of the structure variables is statistically significant in any of the regressions.

Of interest for the pricing strategy discussion is the effect, on the parameter estimates and test statistics, of the inclusion of business assets explicitly into the model. As can be seen, business assets does not replace the loan size variable in terms of partial correlation coefficients (this happened in two of the interest rate regressions in Table 3). But its coefficient is statistically significant in the all customer and noncollateralized customer regressions. The positive sign on the business asset coefficient with other characteristics of the customer, including size of loan, taken into account in the model implies that as businesses increase in size they hold more deposits at their bank. It should be remembered that this variable had a negative coefficient in the interest rate regressions (Table 3). To the extent that deposit balances are an important price, these findings suggest a rationale for the often voiced opinion that larger businesses are preferred bank customers.

Because of the impact of region on interest rates, it is desirable to compute regressions where regional variables are included when deposits are the dependent variable. Regressions on deposit balances, with the six partition regional variable, were, therefore, computed and are shown in Table 8. The *F* tests indicate that all three regressions are statistically significant at the 1 per cent level. As can be seen in Table 8, the inclusion of the regional variable does not alter the dominant relationships observed in Table 7. In the all customer regression, nine variables are statistically significant, eight at the 1 per cent level and one at the 5 per cent level, of which seven variables are customer characteristics. The noncollateralized regression has eleven statistically significant variables, of which seven are customer characteristics. The fully collateralized regression has five statistically significant variables but only two of these variables are customer characteristics. Thus, the customer characteristics are the major determinants of the amount of deposits held.

None of the coefficients of the two branch restriction dummy variables are statistically significant. The coefficient of concentration in the fully collateralized regression is statistically significant at the 5 per cent level; but the sign is negative. We have no explanation for this anomalous result.

To test the influence of business size on the deposit component of bank prices, regressions were run on model 4 on three business size classes. The parameter estimates and test statistics for these regressions are shown in Appendix F. The parameter estimates for the structural variables are shown in Table 9. Because all observations on medium and large sized businesses that fully collateralized their loans in statewide branching markets were in Region 6, these regressions could not be computed. The R^2's for all seven regressions are significant at the 1 per cent level. The signs of the variables and the ranking by size of partial R conform very strongly to the results of the other regressions where deposit is the dependent variable.

As can be seen in Table 9, only two of the twenty-one coefficients of the three structure variables are statistically significant; one at the 1 per cent level and the other at the 5 per cent level. It is interesting to note that both statistically significant coefficients are in the small business size class of the all customer regressions and both coefficients have a negative sign. This suggests that small size business customers in unit bank markets, which have the highest negative coefficients, hold smaller deposits than the same size customers hold in restricted and statewide branching markets and that small size customers in restricted markets hold less balances than are held by small business in statewide branching markets. Although this finding is reasonable in terms of our belief in how markets operate, it is disconcerting in that the coefficients in the noncollateralized and the fully collateralized customer regressions are not statistically significant in either the unit banking or restricted banking markets. Also, the discussion of bank pricing implied that noncollateralized customers are the appropriate group to use in estimating the price-market structure relationship. More-

TABLE 8.   Regressions on Model 4, All Customers in SMSA's, With a Six Partition Regional Variable, Average Deposits Dependent

	All Customers (1)		No Collateral (2)		Collateralized 100 Per Cent or More (3)
Average deposit (mean)	408.44		463.89		274.81
1. Original amount	0.1963	(1)	0.1957	(1)	0.1387
	1244.78		1241.44		1356.90
	32.03a		27.76a		15.04a
	0.35		0.40		.34
2. Account activity	232.27	(2)	247.71	(2)	187.66
	1.84		1.90		1.69
	14.37a		13.08a		7.10a
	0.16		0.20		0.17
3. Other bank	236.31	(3)	237.12	(10)	80.67
	0.26		0.26		0.26
	6.58a		5.43a		1.46
	0.08		0.09		0.04
4. Interest rate	−1.31	(4)	−1.84	(7)	−0.54
	641.57		635.86		655.80
	5.11a		5.07a		1.70
	0.06		0.08		0.04
5. Time in debt	−22.97	(9)	−13.17	(9)	13.87
	10.03		9.71		10.63
	4.61a		2.31b		1.57
	0.05		0.04		0.04
6. Log bank size	131.91	(12)	94.82	(5)	146.89
	6.097		6.1476		6.0450
	3.08a		1.76		2.21b
	0.04		0.03		0.05
7. Length of lending arrangement	65.81	(10)	64.29	(11)	43.77
	2.66		2.69		2.60
	2.59a		2.08b		1.13
	0.03		0.03		0.03
8. Other services	85.41	(5)	170.31	(18)	−10.13
	0.24		0.22		0.25
	2.37a		3.85a		0.18
	0.03		0.06		0.01
9. Region 4	152.63	(8)	222.74	(3)	287.48
	0.23		0.21		0.31
	2.27b		2.64a		2.56b
	0.03		0.04		0.06
10. Population increase	4.16	(7)	7.76	(15)	1.11
	7.47		8.10		6.95
	1.76		2.72a		0.27
	0.02		0.04		0.01

TABLE 8—(*Concluded*)

	All Customers (1)	No Collateral (2)	Collateralized 100 Per Cent or More (3)
11. Region 3	−67.46	(11) −122.83	(6) 164.97
	0.16	0.15	0.16
	1.35	2.06[b]	1.90
	0.02	0.03	0.05
12. Unit bank dummy	−107.43	(18) −10.31	(12) −242.62
	0.34	0.28	0.48
	1.10	0.09	0.77
	0.01	0.01	0.02
13. Region 2	33.11	(6) 170.43	(13) 50.41
	0.15	0.14	0.12
	0.68	2.95[a]	0.58
	0.01	0.05	0.02
14. Region 6	−63.13	(16) 134.27	(17) 67.01
	0.07	0.07	0.07
	0.64	1.25	0.21
	0.01	0.02	0.01
15. Concentration	48.42	(13) 198.13	(4) −460.79
	0.68	0.66	0.69
	0.40	1.38	2.30[b]
	0.01	0.02	0.06
16. Region 5	−26.26	(19) 2.49	(8) 178.04
	0.12	0.08	0.17
	0.37	0.03	1.57
	0.01	0.01	0.04
17. Log total deposits (SMSA)	−9.64	(17) 43.31	(14) −24.07
	5.9879	6.0649	5.9435
	0.27	1.01	0.43
	0.01	0.02	0.01
18. Limited branch dummy	7.99	(14) 114.53	(16) −75.28
	0.55	0.60	0.44
	0.10	1.30	0.25
	0.01	0.02	0.01
19. Deposit fluctuation	0.52	(15) 29.00	(19) −3.38
	1.70	1.72	1.67
	0.03	1.30	0.12
	0.01	0.02	0.01
Intercept	−252.90	−445.46	−275.31
R^2	0.22	0.31	0.21
F	114.03[a]	95.21[a]	23.49[a]
N	7614	4000	1729

NOTE: See the notes to Table 6.

[a] Significant at the .01 level.

[b] Significant at the .05 level.

TABLE 9. Parameter Estimates and Test Statistics for Structural Variables, Customers With Asset Data, Three Size Classes, Deposits Dependent

	Asset Size (millions of dollars)					
		$0 \leq .5$		$.5 \leq 1$		$1 \leq 5$
Unit banking						
All customers	(8)	−70.26	(10)	−67.16	(12)	−211.90
		.34		.35		.36
		2.90[a]		.55		.86
		.05		.02		.03
Noncollateralized	(13)	−26.65	(11)	134.32	(10)	311.96
		.25		.28		.30
		.88		.95		.95
		.02		.05		.05
Collateralized 100 per cent	(16)	−73.10				
or more		.52		c		c
		.45				
		.02				
Restricted branching						
All customers	(12)	−42.68	(19)	−2.29	(16)	−38.00
		.57		.55		.55
		2.17[b]		.02		.17
		.04		.01		.01
Noncollateralized	(11)	−31.28	(9)	150.00	(6)	418.24
		.62		.61		.59
		1.39		1.31		1.56
		.04		.07		.07
Collateralized 100 per cent	(19)	2.03				
or more		.41				
		.01		c		c
		.01				
Concentration						
All customers	(15)	−28.97	(7)	−145.08	(6)	521.25
		.68		.68		.67
		.98		.96		1.79
		.02		.04		.06
Noncollateralized	(16)	−26.50	(6)	330.46		728.41
		.66		.67		.66
		.67		1.72		1.79
		.02		.09		.09
Collateralized 100 per cent	(9)	−135.83				
or more		.70				
		1.34		c		c
		.06				

NOTE: Within each column, the first number is the regression coefficient; the second, the mean; the third, the T value; and the fourth, the partial correlation coefficient. The numbers in parentheses indicate the order of the variables within their respective regressions.

SOURCE: Appendix F.

[a] Significant at the .01 level.
[b] Significant at the .05 level.
[c] These regressions could not be computed because of the sample of customers.

over, the weight of the evidence of the regressions where deposits are the dependent variable suggests that deposit balances are not related to branching restrictions. Thus we conclude that business size does not influence the deposit component of the prices businesses pay for bank services.

In conclusion, the evidence from the regressions with mean deposit balance as the dependent variable implies that market structure variables do not affect the quantity of deposits held by business customers. Deposits maintained are primarily a function of the characteristics of the bank-business relationship.

The data suggest that size of bank has some influence on the level of deposits, but other characteristics, such as variations in demand between markets and size of markets, do not have a statistically measurable influence. Thus, it is concluded that the deposit component of the vector of bank prices in the bank-customer relationship is not affected by market structure variables, but rather seems to be applied uniformly across markets.

Chapter 4

CONCLUSIONS

THIS PAPER attempted to empirically estimate the relationship between the prices banks charge businesses for services rendered and the structure of bank markets. A model of bank pricing was developed which implied that banks utilize a package or customer pricing strategy because of the regulatory prohibition on the payment of interest on demand deposits and because of profit maximization criteria. Banks supply customers with a number of services and are paid through a mixture of three types of prices: interest rates on loans, deposit balances, and fees. It is impossible to measure the relative importance of these three prices because the deposit element of the price vector causes a reduction in costs, whereas interest payments and fees are additions to revenues received by the bank.[1]

Although proportions cannot be measured directly, it must be presumed that, in terms of costs, interest payments are the most important price of bank services to most businesses. In terms of revenues received, interest rates are the most important price to most banks. But, the deposit balance is also a cost

[1] Some insights into the relative size of interest and deposit payments can be gained from all bank revenue and expense data for 1967. Interest expense for savings, time deposits, and other purchased money was approximately 45 per cent of the $16.6 billion total operating expenses. Purchased funds accounted for less than 48 per cent of total deposits of $398 billion. Thus, banks bartered services for more than half of their nonequity funds. In acquiring these funds, they incurred actual costs which accounted for a substantial portion of the 55 per cent of total operating expenses not directly attributed to purchasing funds and an undetermined amount of opportunity costs which reduced fee and interest income. During 1967, interest and discounts earned on loans accounted for approximately two-thirds and interest on securities and investments one-fifth of the $21.8 billion of operating revenue of all banks. Income earned through fees and service charges were a relatively minor source of measured income for commercial banks in 1967.

to businesses and an important revenue to banks. The statements above refer to the banking system as a whole. It is recognized that the proportion of cost to the business between interest payments and income foregone to maintain deposits and, therefore, contribution to the revenue of the individual bank, depends on the relative importance of loans and other bank services in the package of services provided by the bank.[2] Fee income is, however, a relatively minor source of bank compensation.

To estimate the influence of bank market structure on loan rates and deposit balances two models were developed and their parameters estimated. The values and signs of the coefficients of the market structure variables suggest the general conclusion that branching restrictions and the degree of concentration are positively associated with interest rates; interest rates rise with tightened branch restrictions and rise with increases in the concentration of ownership of bank deposits in a market. More particularly, the evidence suggests that small firms, those with up to one-half million dollars in assessts, pay higher loan rates as branching restrictions are tightened. But, branching restrictions do not have a statistically significant effect on firms above this size. The level of market concentration has a statistically significant impact on rates paid by firms with assets up to at least $5 million.

The import of these conclusions for public policy should be evaluated with the expected size of the impact of variations in market structure on interest rates taken into account. Since different parameter estimates of the structural variables were computed for different sets of customers, it is difficult to generalize. Nonetheless, accepting the "All Customer" regression in Table 5, derived from Appendix Table D-1 as the appropriate estimate for all customers, the following statements about the

[2] There are many businesses where interest payments are the minor cost and deposits and fees are the major payment; for instance, food chains and other stores deposit large numbers of checks and do not borrow heavily from banks. Banks usually charge for such activity through deposit requirements and less frequently through fees.

impact of changes in concentration and branch restrictions are implied. If concentration in a market increased to 74 per cent (or 10 per cent from the computed mean of approximately 67 per cent), the mean loan rate for firms with below a half million dollars in assets would be expected to increase from 6.53 to 6.58; a decline of 10 per cent to 60 per cent would be expected to cause a reduction in the mean loan rate to 6.48 per cent. For firms with assets between a half million and a million dollars, rates would change from 6.38 to 6.42 and from 6.38 to 6.34. For larger firms, those with between one and five million dollars in assets, 10 per cent changes in concentration would change rates from 6.28 to 6.33 and from 6.28 to 6.23.

The expected difference in rates for firms with up to a half million dollars in assets between statewide branching and unit banking markets is 33 basis points. For these smaller firms the movement from restricted to statewide branching markets is expected to increase loan rates 13 basis points. But the evidence suggests that the rates paid by firms with assets above a half million dollars are not expected to be affected by changes in branching restrictions.

The magnitude of changes in loan rates implied by variations in the level of market concentration, less than 5 basis points for a 10 per cent change in market concentration, is almost insignificant in relation to the mean rates of 653 basis points for the smallest firms or even the 627 basis points mean rate of the largest firms.[3] The possible change in rates implied by alterations in branching restrictions, 33 basis points for the change from unit to statewide branching and 13 basis points for a change from restricted to statewide branching, each of which has far reaching implications on the structure of banking markets with regard

---

[3] It is interesting to note that the estimates of the effects of changes in concentration on loan rates is close to, but below, the estimates reported by Edwards and Phillips. Edwards reported that a 10 per cent increase in concentration would increase loan rates 6 basis points, Edwards, *op. cit.*, p. 90. Phillips said that a 10 per cent increase in concentration would increase loan rates 8 basis points, Phillips, *op. cit.*, p. 924. But it should be remembered that Edwards did not include a regional variable in his model and his data contained errors due to weighting. Phillips' estimates were produced from quarterly loan surveys, which is an entirely different body of data.

to number of offices and number of banks, is also not quantitatively very significant.

The conclusions concerning the relationship of deposit balances to the market structure variables are much more straightforward than the loan rate relationship. Deposit balances are not affected by variations in the concentration of ownership of bank deposits in the market or the degree of branching restrictions.

When these two sets of findings are combined, it is concluded that variations in structure probably affect the "price" of the package of services provided business customers, and the relationship is positive for both concentration and branching restrictions. But the absolute price differences are not of a magnitude to significantly affect the allocation of resources.

Prior studies that reported approximately the same positive impact of the level of concentration on interest rates on loans overstated the quantitative importance of the relationship because the "deposit" price was not incorporated in the analysis.

Although the major focus of this paper was on the estimates of the market-structure–price relationship, the parameter estimates in the regressions contain important insights into bank pricing practices that should at least be mentioned. Their value is due in large measure to the unique body of data collected and analyzed in this study.

The regression estimates lend strong support to the package pricing hypothesis. Both prices, interest rates and deposit balances, were found to be modified by the characteristics of the customer's relationship with the bank. The statistical tests presented suggest that the deposit component of the price vector is almost exclusively affected by the customer characteristics; whereas the loan rate is strongly affected by demand, region, and other elements not directly attributable to the customer.

The signs of size of bank market and size of bank in the interest rate regression suggest the possibility that some of the often reported simple relationships with loan rates may be caused by other variables not usually included in the analysis. The results of more extensive estimates and tests of these hypotheses about bank pricing practices will be reported in a forthcoming study.

Appendix A

QUESTIONNAIRE FOR THE SAMPLE OF LOANS FOR COMMERCIAL AND INDUSTRIAL PURPOSES

Sample of Loans for Commercial and Industrial Purposes

I. LOAN CHARACTERISTICS

1. Amount outstanding on 2/28/67
2. Original amount of current outstanding
3. Interest rate face of note
4. Repayment method (one from Group A)
5. Participation with another bank (Group B)
6. Maximum amount of loans outstanding to this borrower in last 12 months
7. Is loan collateralized? If yes, estimate current collateral value relative to maximum loan balance (Group C)
8. If (7) yes, is collateral easily marketable. Yes? No?
9. If (7) yes, is any explicit payment made for investigating or handling collateral. Yes? No?
10. Does borrower have outstanding loan(s) from other banks Yes? No?

II. BORROWER CHARACTERISTICS

11. Form of bus. organ. (I) Inc. (U) Uninc.
12. Business of borrower (Group D) Insert letter which best fits
13. Total assets fiscal or calendar year ending in   1966 ___ 1965 ___ 1964 ___ 1963 ___

15. Current liabilities fiscal or calendar year ending   1966 ___ 1965 ___ 1964 ___ 1963 ___
16. Net profits before taxes, fiscal or calendar year ending   1966 ___ 1965 ___ 1964 ___ 1963 ___
17. Net worth, fiscal or calendar year ending   1966 ___ 1965 ___ 1964 ___ 1963 ___

III. CUSTOMER CHARACTERISTICS

18. During the year the fluctuation (High to Low) in this customer's demand deposit balance is (Group E)
19. Average dep. balance last 12 months
20. Length of time this bank has had lending arrangement with this customer (Group F)
21. Length of time during last 12 months borrower was in debt to the bank (in months)
22. This customer's account activity, number of checks written & deposits made is: (Group G)

14. Current assets fiscal or calendar year ending

1966 _____
1965 _____
1964 _____
1963 _____

23. Does bank perform services other than lending and checking for borrower? Yes? No?

24. If (23) yes, does bank make separate charge for these services? Yes? No?

25. If (24) yes, would you estimate the net profit to the bank from providing other services to this customer, fees minus cost of providing services to be: (Group H)

NOTE: Space was provided in the original questionnaire for information on sixteen borrowers for each question. Groups A through H are listed below.

Group A: (a) Single payment; (b) Paid in installments with interest added on; (c) Paid in installments with interest charged on unpaid balance.

Group B: (a) No; (b) Originated with your bank; (c) Originated with another bank; (d) Pool type participation.

Group C: (a) No; (b) 50 per cent or less, (c) 51 to 75 per cent; (d) 76 to 99 per cent; (e) 100 per cent or more.

Group D: (a) Manufacturing and mining; (b) Wholesale trade and distributors, (c) Retail trade; (d) Commodity, bond, and stock dealers—members of recognized exchange; (e) Finance companies—Sales, small loan and commercial; (f) Real estate and construction—Does not include mortgage financing; (g) Service firms—Repair services, medical and dental, legal and other; (h) All others, specify.

Group E: (a) Very small; (b) Moderate; (c) Very wide.

Group F: (a) Less than 1 year; (b) 1 through 3 years; (c) More than 3 years.

Group G: (a) Small; (b) Moderate; (c) Large; (d) Very large.

Group H: (a) Losses; (b) Break even; (c) Some profit; (d) Highly profitable.

Appendix B

THE SAMPLE OF BANK
CUSTOMER PROFILES

Appendix B

THIS APPENDIX describes the bank customer profile data used in the empirical sections of this study. A sample of banks were requested to supply data describing the characteristics of a number of their borrowing customers. A copy of the questionnaire and the instructions which accompanied the questionnaire are shown in Appendix A. Banks were chosen from among the population of all banks in the three asset sizes: $40–$60 million, $80–$120 million, and $200–400 million. A small proportion of the banks in these size classes domiciled outside of SMSA's were sampled; almost all banks in these size classes domiciled in SMSA's were sent requests for data. The banks were chosen at random from the SMSA's that had a very large number of banks with assets between $40–$400 million. The goal was to have representation from as large a number of SMSA's as possible, with a distribution among the three types of branch restrictions. Responses were received from 160 banks domiciled in 107 SMSA's. Appendix Table B-1 shows the distribution of responding banks by type of bank organization, whether unit or branch, and by degree of branching restriction. The distribution of responding banks by asset size and SMSA designation is shown in Appendix Table B-2.

The largest banks were requested to supply 80 customer profiles, the middle size banks were asked to supply 60 customers,

Appendix Table B-1

Number of Branch and Unit Banks by State and Branching Regulation

State Code	Within SMSA		Outside SMSA	
	Branch	Unit	Branch	Unit
Unit	7	47	0	6
Restricted branching	73	5	4	0
Statewide branching	13	4	1	0

Appendix Table B-2
Location and Size Class of Responding Banks

SMSA	Total Number of Banks	Number of Banks With Assets of		
		$40–$60 Million	$80–$120 Million	$200–$400 Million
000	11	5	5	1
002	1	0	1	0
005	1	1	0	0
008	1	0	0	1
010	1	0	1	0
012	1	0	0	1
013	1	0	1	0
015	1	0	1	0
017	1	0	0	1
018	4	3	1	0
019	1	0	0	1
022	1	0	1	0
023	1	1	0	0
024	1	0	0	1
025	2	0	2	0
027	1	0	0	1
028	8	3	3	2
030	2	1	1	0
033	2	0	0	2
034	1	1	0	0
037	1	0	0	1
040	2	0	1	1
042	1	1	0	0
043	1	0	1	0
046	2	1	1	0
047	2	0	2	0
048	1	1	0	0
052	1	0	0	1
057	1	1	0	0
059	1	1	0	0
060	1	1	0	0
062	1	1	0	0
065	1	1	0	0
069	2	0	0	2
070	1	1	0	0

Appendix Table B-2-(*Continued*)

SMSA	Total Number of Banks	Number of Banks With Assets of		
		$40–$60 Million	$80–$120 Million	$200–$400 Million
071	1	0	1	0
072	1	0	1	0
073	1	0	0	1
076	2	1	1	0
077	1	0	1	0
078	1	1	0	0
081	1	1	0	0
082	1	0	1	0
083	1	0	1	0
084	1	1	0	0
086	2	0	0	2
088	2	1	1	0
090	1	0	1	0
095	2	1	1	0
096	1	0	1	0
100	1	0	0	1
102	1	1	0	0
104	1	0	0	1
105	1	1	0	0
108	1	1	0	0
109	1	1	0	0
110	1	1	0	0
112	5	2	0	3
114	1	1	0	0
117	2	0	2	0
119	1	1	0	0
120	1	1	0	0
121	1	1	0	0
123	1	0	0	1
124	1	0	0	1
125	1	1	0	0
126	1	0	0	1
127	1	0	1	0
131	2	1	0	1
132	2	0	0	2
133	1	1	0	0

(*Continued*)

Appendix Table B-2-(*Concluded*)

SMSA	Total Number of Banks	Number of Banks With Assets of		
		$40–$60 Million	$80–$120 Million	$200–$400 Million
136	1	0	1	0
137	1	0	0	1
141	1	1	0	0
142	1	0	0	1
143	3	1	1	1
147	1	0	1	0
149	2	0	2	0
155	1	0	0	1
156	1	0	0	1
159	3	2	0	1
160	1	0	1	0
161	3	1	1	1
163	1	0	0	1
165	2	0	2	0
166	1	0	0	1
167	1	1	0	0
168	2	2	0	0
171	1	0	1	0
173	1	0	1	0
176	2	0	1	1
177	1	0	1	0
178	3	0	3	0
179	1	1	0	0
183	1	0	1	0
185	1	0	1	0
188	1	0	0	1
189	1	0	1	0
190	3	1	2	0
191	4	0	1	3
192	1	1	0	0
194	1	1	0	0
197	1	1	0	0
201	1	1	0	0
202	1	0	1	0
203	1	1	0	0
205	1	0	1	0
209	1	0	1	0
216	1	1	0	0
220	1	0	1	0
223	1	1	0	0

and the smallest banks were asked for 40 customers. The coded questionnaires produced 8,157 customer profiles which have been used in the estimates and statistical tests in this study. The number of customer profiles by SMSA is shown in Appendix Table B-3.

Appendix Table B-3
Number of Customer Profiles by SMSA

SMSA	Number of Customers	SMSA	Number of Customers
2	32	70	25
5	40	71	52
8	77	72	62
10	64	73	79
12	55	76	95
13	60	77	48
15	64	78	42
17	76	81	40
18	153	83	58
19	79	84	43
22	60	86	156
23	40	88	99
24	80	90	23
25	100	95	85
27	71	96	58
28	341	100	30
30	51	102	40
33	126	104	80
34	40	108	31
37	78	109	39
40	139	110	41
42	40	112	221
43	60	114	40
46	106	117	64
47	106	119	40
48	40	120	33
52	80	121	14
57	40	123	80
59	40	124	79
60	39	125	40
62	39	126	56
65	40	127	54
69	159	131	90

(Continued)

Appendix Table B-3-(*Concluded*)

SMSA	Number of Customers	SMSA	Number of Customers
132	120	173	11
133	40	176	142
136	56	177	30
137	76	178	115
141	40	183	41
142	29	185	60
143	132	188	63
147	59	189	46
149	113	190	116
155	80	191	293
156	80	192	46
159	160	194	40
160	60	197	35
161	182	201	40
163	80	202	60
165	119	203	16
166	85	205	51
167	16	209	64
168	40	216	40
171	64	223	16

Some requests for clarification of responses were sent to banks but generally when particular customer profiles were not complete in a number of key variables, e.g., when no loan data was provided, or the data were obviously inconsistent, the customer was dropped from the sample. This is the major reason for the odd number of customers in some SMSA's. In a number of instances, however, banks supplied more or less customers than were requested.

Bank files do not contain balance sheet or income statements for many customers. The lack of these data did not cause the customers to be dropped from the sample. Of the 8,157 customer profiles in the sample only 5,265 have business asset figures for 1965 (see Appendix Table B-4).

Thus, the sample of customer profiles contains different numbers of observations when the purpose for which it is used changes. If the focus is upon the supply of bank services to

Appendix Table B-4

Number of Customer Profiles by Data Partition

Customers		
Total		8,157
In SMSA's	7,614	
Outside of SMSA's	543	
With business assets		5,265
In SMSA's	4,957	
Outside of SMSA's	308	
With more than one bank		2,112
In SMSA's	1,987	
Outside of SMSA's	125	
With no collateral		4,213
With any collateral		2,714
With collateral greater than		
100 per cent	1,861	
With collateral blank		1,230

business and only customer characteristics at the bank are considered, all observations, both in SMSA's and outside SMSA's, can be used. The sample size for this analysis would be the full 8,157 customers. If the analysis also considers bank market characteristics, only customers of banks domiciled in an SMSA can be used and the sample is 7,614. When business asset size is used the sample declines to 5,265, and if market variables and business assets are used in the same equation the sample is 4,957. Sample sizes by these and other partitions can be seen in the data contained in Appendix Table B-4.

To keep the customer profiles as homogenous as possible, banks were instructed to include only short-term borrowers. This request was aimed at reducing the price variability because of difference in the original maturity of the loan. Customers were to be chosen from those who had received their loan after the last prime rate change or who had their loan rate renegotiated after the last change. There is some indication that this request was heeded by bankers, since a number of respondents included fewer than the requested number of customers and noted that this number was 100 per cent of their business customers that fell into the above category. Moreover, this requirement brought a large number of requests for clarification from bankers. But most probably the sample is not completely homogenous in this dimension.

Some indication of the potential problem of heterogeneous rate, because of differences in the date the rate was negotiated during a period of changing rates, is given by the distribution of customer time in debt during the last twelve months (see Appendix Table B-5). Seventy-six per cent of the customers

Appendix Table B-5
Length of Time During Last Twelve Months
Customer Was in Debt to Bank

Months	Number of Customers	Percentage
1	214	03
2	176	02
3	213	03
4	181	02
5	194	02
6	361	04
7	251	03
8	329	04
9	360	04
10	403	05
11	445	05
12	5,019	62
Blank	11	00

included in the sample were in debt to their bank for nine or more months in the twelve months preceding the survey date. It is possible that a substantial fraction of the customers in debt for a major part of the year renewed their notes periodically or that the rate was tied to the prime rate. But, there is certainly reason to believe that some error in variable exists in the loan rate data, if this rate is meant to depict the rate accorded to short-term loans granted at the time the survey was conducted. The survey was taken about a month after the prime bank rate had fallen from 6 per cent to 5.75 per cent. Thus, there is probably some upward bias in the interest rates in some of the customer profiles. It should be noted that this potential bias is most troublesome for direct comparisons of rates or distributions of rates. For the major purpose for which these data are used, in regressions with other customer profile variables, concern about this bias is reduced. There is no reason to believe the bias is not randomly distributed with regard to the structural variables.

The nature of the data requested reduced concern about bias being introduced by bankers purposefully choosing customers to include in the sample. Moreover, bankers were asked for a substantial body of data that was time consuming and difficult to supply. Thus, no complicated sampling procedures could be attempted. Nonetheless some simple rules were given for the sample of customers to be included from among the eligible customers (see the instructions in the questionnaire in Appendix A). The major bias in this regard is probably due to the desire of bankers to supply data for all boxes in the questionnaire for the customers included. Bankers, therefore, would be expected to choose customers for whom their files were most complete. The replies indicating that many small banks were hard put to supply the requested number of customers, even when all eligible customers were listed, precluded any sophisticated sampling design.

Banks were asked to give the interest rate on the face of the note and indicate the method of repayment in separate questions. The effective loan rate was then computed from the responses to these two questions. Considerable correspondence was required to clarify these data to assure that interest rates were properly stated.

The periodic Federal Reserve Business Loan Surveys and the Quarterly Survey of Interest Rates on Short & Intermediate Term Loans request data on loan rates and amount of loan outstanding on the survey data. Such data have serious shortcomings as estimates of the current interest price bank borrowers must pay for loans. The interest rates observed on loans in the banks portfolio at any moment of time depend on the date the notes were written and the recent movement in interest rates. The computed average rate depends on these two factors and the mix of the customer population that happens to be in debt to the bank at the time the survey is conducted. In addition to the problems of timing and mix, one of the major hypotheses of this study, that banks price their services on a package basis, implies that the current loan outstanding when the survey is taken is not the appropriate measure of the loan on which the price is based. The bank pricing model implies that the maximum loan which the bank expects to be called upon to grant the customer is an important determinant of the loan price; however, pretesting of the questionnaire with a number of banks demonstrated that a request for an estimate of the maximum loan which would be made could rarely be specified. Bankers demonstrated an aversion to estimating any number, especially one which was in dollars and essentially unconstrained. It was even difficult to get estimates where a choice of three or four possibilities was listed. In an attempt to develop data to represent the expected maximum loan, the questionnaire requested three loan size parameters, the current loan outstanding (question 1), the original amount of the currently outstanding loan (question 2), and the maximum amount of loans outstanding to this borrower in the last twelve months (question 6). The distribution of these three variables is shown in Appendix Table B-6. As can be seen there is no substantial difference between the three measures of loans outstanding, which suggests that any of the alternate loan measures will not prove a substantial improvement as a proxy for the theoretically correct loan variable.

The deposit size distribution of the customer profiles is shown in Appendix Table B-7. Of major interest is the fact that only 10 per cent of the customers with loans outstanding did not have deposits with the bank during the preceding twelve months. The presumption is, of course, that this is a good estimate of the proportion of business customers who do not have deposits with the bank from whom they borrow.

The distribution of the ratio of deposits to outstanding loans

Appendix Table B-6
Size of Loan, Number, and Percentage Distribution

Loan Size (dollars)	Current Loan Outstanding		Maximum Loan Outstanding		Original Loan Outstanding	
	Number	Percentage	Number	Percentage	Number	Percentage
1- 10,000	2,569	31	2,552	31	2,284	28
10,001- 20,000	1,154	14	898	11	1,111	14
20,001- 40,000	1,124	14	1,146	14	1,177	14
40,001- 80,000	1,029	13	1,263	15	1,090	13
80,001-120,000	516	06	481	06	551	07
120,001-200,000	618	08	556	07	683	08
200,001-400,000	602	07	627	08	640	08
400,001 <	545	07	634	08	621	08

Appendix Table B-7
Distribution of Customers by Deposit Size

Deposit Size (dollars)	Number of Customers	Percentage
0	801	10
1– 2,500	1,595	20
2,501– 5,000	980	12
5,001– 10,000	1,047	13
10,001– 20,000	1,126	14
20,001– 40,000	936	11
40,001– 60,000	497	06
60,001– 80,000	315	04
80,001–100,000	202	02
100,001 <	658	08

by asset size of business is shown in Appendix Table B-8. The ratios are partitioned into three groups, 30 per cent or less, greater than 30 per cent and less than 60 per cent, and greater than 60 per cent; collateralized and noncollateralized customers are shown separately. As size of firm increases, the ratios change very markedly. As expected, the changes are most pronounced for the noncollateralized customers. Among customers that collateralize their loan, the smallest sized firms are less than half as likely to be in 0–30 per cent deposit to loan category than the very largest firms and are three times more likely than the largest firms to be in the 60 per cent and over category. Although the differences are much less substantial for collateralized customers, the same pattern exists. It is interesting to note that the ratio of loans to deposits for all customers is not greatly different from this ratio for customers with asset size data.

As can be seen in Appendix Table B-4, 2,714 customers collateralized their loans. Of this number the collateral of 1,861 customers was considered to be greater than 100 per cent of the loan. Collateral can have many forms, with varying costs associated with handling and varying degrees of reduction in risk exposure. Collateral which is readily marketable affords the bank the maximum reduction in risk per dollar of collateral. Moreover, marketable collateral consists mainly of securities and

Appendix Table B-8

Distribution of the Ratio of Average Deposit Balance to Outstanding Loan, by Size of Firm and All Customers

Firm Size (dollars)	Percentage of Noncollateralized Customers With a Deposit-Outstanding Ratio of			Percentage of Collateralized Customers With a Deposit-Outstanding Ratio of			Percentage of All Customers With a Deposit-Outstanding Ratio of		
	0-30 Per Cent	31-60 Per Cent	>60 Per Cent	0-30 Per Cent	31-60 Per Cent	>60 Per Cent	0-30 Per Cent	31-60 Per Cent	>60 Per Cent
0- 100,000	34.75	25.79	39.48	51.62	23.10	25.28	40.47	22.08	37.46
100,001- 250,000	37.86	21.10	41.04	62.43	15.61	21.95	47.51	18.37	34.12
250,001- 500,000	37.95	24.12	37.94	64.31	17.04	18.65	50.59	19.58	29.85
500,001- 1,000,000	45.09	18.85	36.07	62.97	17.17	19.84	52.98	18.15	28.86
1,000,001- 5,000,000	51.85	19.74	28.42	65.80	16.73	17.48	56.88	17.68	25.44
5,000,001- 20,000,000	57.66	16.56	25.76	71.15	9.62	19.24	61.57	12.54	25.89
20,000,001 <	71.95	15.84	12.22	73.68	15.78	10.53	71.48	15.63	12.89
Total with asset data	44.26	21.33	34.40	61.99	17.43	20.56	50.88	18.69	30.40
All customers	45.33	20.35	34.32	65.70	16.21	18.09	54.18	18.42	27.40

bonds, which are usually the least costly to handle. It is, therefore, significant that the collateral of only 19 per cent of the
collateralized loan customers was considered easily marketable
by their banks. Thus, the loans of four-fifths of the customers
that maintained some collateral as backing of their loans still
had some elements of risk to the bank. Of interest also is the
fact that only 3 per cent of the customers that presented collateral were charged an investigating and handling fee. This
suggests these costs are mainly recaptured through interest
charges on loans and in other revenues from the relationship.

In general a balance that fluctuates is less valuable to the
bank than one that is more stable. The distribution of replies
to question 18, which requested a qualitative judgment about
the fluctuation of the deposit balance, is shown in Appendix
Table B-9. The deposit balance of 42 per cent of the customers

Appendix Table B-9
Fluctuation in Deposit Balance

Deposit Fluctuation	Number of Customers	Percentage
Very small	2,221	27
Moderate	3,438	42
Very wide	1,592	20
Blank	906	11

fluctuated moderately; something more than a quarter of the
customers had a very small fluctuation; 20 per cent fluctuated
very widely. The 11 per cent nonresponse is explained largely
by the fact that approximately 10 per cent of the customers
did not have deposits. Some customers, however, may have ab-
solutely stable deposit balances; mainly customers whose deposit
is the minimum required compensating balance. But the majority of the extra 1 per cent must be attributed to nonresponse
to a qualitative question.

The expected stability of the bank-customer relationship is
borne out by the replies to question 20, shown in Appendix
Table B-10. Three-fourths of the customers had been with the

Appendix Table B-10
Distribution of Length of Customer Lending Arrangement

Length of Lending Arrangement	Number of Customers	Percentage
Less than one year	718	09
One through three years	1,296	16
More than three years	6,138	75
Blank	5	00

bank for more than three years. Less than 10 per cent were customers for less than a year.

Account activity of the customer is an important measure of the services performed by the bank. But activity has a number of components, such as deposits, checks, currency and coins supplied and/or counted, and returned items. Therefore, a qualitative measure was the only feasible method of describing this variable. The distribution of responses to question 22, which probed this element of the customer relationship, is shown in Appendix Table B-11. One-quarter of the customers had large

Appendix Table B-11
Distribution of Customer Account Activity

Account Activity	Number of Customers	Percentage
Small	2,215	27
Moderate	3,095	38
Large	1,469	18
Very large	549	07
Blank	829	10

or very large amounts of activity and, therefore, this element of the relationship must have been considered an important component of the revenue that the bank expected to receive from these customers. About a quarter of the customers were considered by the bank to have a small amount of activity and more than 40 per cent had moderate activity.

It is, of course, well understood by both bankers and customers that services are bartered for deposit balances. In large measure the services purchased are loans and deposit related activity. An unknown fraction of bank customers purchase additional services, which are paid for with deposits or explicit fees. Questions 23–25 developed information about this element of the business-customer–bank relationship. Twenty-four per cent of customers in the sample receive services other than borrowing and fund transfer from their banks. Approximately 80 per cent of these customers pay for these services by separate charges. Unfortunately, the questionnaire did not probe into the distribution of these charges between balances and fees.

The distribution of answers to question 25, which requested a qualitative evaluation of the profitability of charges made for these services, is shown in Appendix Table B-12. As can be

Appendix Table B-12
Estimate of Net Profit to Bank of Providing Other Service s

Profitability	Number of Customers	Percentage
Losses	122	07
Break even	476	29
Some profit	857	54
Highly profitable	160	10

seen, 64 per cent of these customers are considered to provide net profit from these services, whereas only 7 per cent are considered to cause a loss.

Appendix C

FORMS OF BANKING ORGANIZATION

FORMS OF BANKING ORGANIZATION

REGION 1

REGION 2

REGION 3

REGION 4

REGION 5

REGION 6

STATEWIDE BRANCH BANKING

LIMITED BRANCH BANKING

UNIT BANKING

NOTE— HEAVY LINES INDICATE STATISTICAL REGIONS, AS REFERRED TO ON P. 46

Appendix D

REGRESSIONS ON MODEL 3

Appendix Table D-1

Regressions on Model 3, All Customers With Asset Data, Three Size Classes, With A Six Partition Regional Variable, Interest Rate Dependent

	Asset Size (millions of dollars)				
	$0 \leq .5$		$.5 \leq 1$		$1 \leq 5$
Interest rate (mean)	6.527		6.383		6.275
1. Region 6	1.0018	(2)	.5418	(1)	.7586
	.05		.07		.07
	14.04[a]		3.68[a]		6.22[a]
	.25		.14		.21
2. Population increase	.0148	(1)	.0156	(4)	.0105
	7.36		7.26		7.02
	8.06[a]		4.16[a]		3.85[a]
	.15		.16		.13
3. Concentration	.4813	(4)	.4107	(8)	.4752
	.67		.68		.67
	5.62[a]		2.27[b]		3.37[a]
	.10		.09		.12
4. Log total deposits (SMSA)	.1362	(6)	.1024	(3)	.1718
	1.9893		1.9990		2.0124
	5.35[a]		1.88		3.97[a]
	.10		.07		.14
5. Unit bank dummy	.3397	(13)	.0987	(14)	.1236
	.34		.35		.36
	4.80[a]		.67		1.03
	.09		.03		.04
6. Log original amount	−.0933	(16)	−.0196	(11)	−.0703
	2.2420		2.8376		3.1857
	4.21[a]		.42		1.92
	.08		.02		.07
7. Average deposit	−2.2204	(3)	−1.1701	(9)	−.5081
	.0118		.0374		.0773
	4.04[a]		2.56[b]		3.00[a]
	.08		.10		.11
8. Deposit fluctuation	.0403	(7)	.0470	(19)	.0030
	1.73		1.85		1.87
	3.08[a]		1.82		.15
	.06		.07		.01
9. Region 5	.1500	(18)	.0186	(6)	.2790
	.12		.12		.10
	2.98[a]		.19		3.50[a]
	.06		.01		.12
10. Region 4	.1411	(5)	.1706	(2)	.3952
	.23		.26		.29
	2.93[a]		1.97[b]		5.97[a]
	.05		.07		.21

Appendix Table D-1—(*Concluded*)

	Asset Size (millions of dollars)				
	0 ≤ .5		.5 ≤ 1		1 ≤ 5
11. Other services	−.0699	(14)	−.0243	(16)	−.0150
	.23		.28		.30
	2.67[a]		.51		.40
	.05		.02		.01
12. Length of lending arrangement	−.0429	(12)	−.0309	(7)	−.1126
	2.65		2.79		2.77
	2.40[b]		.67		3.41[a]
	.04		.03		.12
13. Limited branch dummy	.1285	(19)	.0020	(12)	.1680
	.56		.55		.55
	2.23[b]		.02		1.58
	.04		.01		.06
14. Region 2	.0706	(17)	−.0289	(13)	.0798
	.17		.12		.11
	2.07[b]		.38		1.31
	.04		.01		.05
15. Region 3	−.0354	(10)	−.0974	(10)	.1348
	.14		.16		.19
	.95		1.35		2.50[b]
	.02		.05		.09
16. Other bank	−.0157	(11)	.0420	(15)	.0234
	.14		.27		.42
	.50		.83		.66
	.01		.03		.02
17. Time in debt	−.0018	(9)	.0130	(5)	.0210
	9.95		10.56		10.29
	.49		1.53		3.50[a]
	.01		.06		.12
18. Log bank size	−.0114	(8)	−.1195	(18)	−.0103
	2.0649		2.1143		2.1664
	.36		1.81		.19
	.01		.07		.01
19. Account activity	.0041	(15)	−.0105	(17)	.0032
	1.79		2.07		2.20
	.32		.44		.19
	.01		.02		.01
Intercept	5.854		5.915		5.537
R^2	.21		.14		.20
F	40.27[a]		6.09[a]		10.91[a]
N	2868		712		827

NOTE: See the notes to Table 2.

[a] Significant at the .01 level.

[b] Significant at the .05 level.

Appendix Table D-2

Regressions on Model 3, All Noncollateralized Customers With Asset Data, Three Size Classes, With a Six Partition Regional Variable, Interest Rate Dependent

	Asset Size (millions of dollars)				
	0 ≤ .5		.5 ≤ 1		1 ≤ 5
Interest rate (mean)	6.484		6.272		6.217
1. Region 6	1.0272	(1)	.6875	(1)	.7645
	.06		.06		.07
	14.18[a]		5.00[a]		6.48[a]
	.34		.26		.30
2. Log original amount	−.1946	(4)	−.1284	(4)	−.1459
	2.1471		2.7556		3.1305
	7.22[a]		2.50[b]		3.5001[a]
	.18		.13		−.17
3. Population increase	.0110	(3)	.0170	(19)	−.0001
	8.06		7.83		7.30
	4.86[a]		3.72		.04
	.12		.20		.01
4. Unit bank dummy	.3423	(11)	.2407	(17)	.0481
	.25		.28		.30
	4.36[a]		1.70		.38
	.11		.09		.02
5. Region 2	.1334	(18)	.0215	(8)	.1251
	.15		.14		.12
	3.42[a]		.29		1.96
	.09		.02		.09
6. Log total deposits (SMSA)	.0945	(10)	.0934	(3)	.1808
	2.0856		2.0855		2.0842
	3.30[a]		1.72		3.96[a]
	.08		.09		.19
7. Concentration	.3228	(6)	.4046	(5)	.4503
	.66		.67		.66
	3.17[a]		2.10[b]		2.93[a]
	.08		.11		.14
8. Average deposit	−1.8760	(8)	−1.0076	(10)	−.2742
	.0126		.0409		.0812
	2.78[a]		1.85		1.54
	.07		.16		.07
9. Deposit fluctuation	.0397	(9)	.0459	(18)	.0023
	1.74		1.89		1.86
	2.55[b]		1.73		.10
	.07		.09		.01
10. Other services	−.0577	(15)	−.0328	(12)	−.0630
	.20		.28		.33
	1.83		.65		1.48
	.05		.04		.07

Appendix Table D-2—(*Concluded*)

	Asset Size (millions of dollars)		
	0 ≤ .5	.5 ≤ 1	1 ≤ 5
11. Limited branch dummy	.0948 (14)	.0976 (16)	.0910
	.62	.61	.59
	1.62	.84	.89
	.04	.05	.04
12. Region 5	.0947 (19)	.0174 (6)	.2965
	.08	.08	.08
	1.47	.16	2.90[a]
	.04	.01	.14
13. Region 4	.0720 (16)	.0377 (2)	.3399
	.20	.24	.26
	1.24	.41	4.63[a]
	.03	.02	.22
14. Time in debt	−.0036 (12)	.0085 (7)	.0130
	9.62	10.18	9.96
	.90	1.08	2.08[b]
	.02	.06	.10
15. Log bank size	.3414 (17)	.0281 (15)	−.0711
	2.1135	2.1854	2.1950
	.85	.40	1.16
	.02	.02	.06
16. Other bank	.0229 (2)	.2225 (9)	.0710
	.11	.24	.42
	.59	3.99[a]	1.82
	.02	.21	.09
17. Account activity	.0078 (7)	−.0491 (11)	−.0279
	1.82	2.14	2.21
	.54	2.00[b]	1.52
	.01	.11	.07
18. Length of lending arrangement	−.0033 (13)	.0480 (13)	−.0488
	2.67	2.82	2.77
	.16	.93	1.37
	.01	.05	.07
19. Region 3	.0005 (5)	−.1762 (6)	.2965
	.12	.14	.08
	.01	2.36[b]	2.90[a]
	.01	.13	.14
Intercept	6.078	5.601	5.973
R^2	.28	.30	.30
F	31.46[a]	7.62[a]	9.50[a]
N	1530	360	449

NOTE: See the notes to Table 2.

[a] Significant at the .01 level.

[b] Significant at the .05 level.

Appendix D

Appendix Table D-3

Regressions on Model 3, All Fully Collateralized Customers With Assets Less Than or Equal to $½ Million, With a Six Partition Regional Variable, Interest Rate Dependent.

Interest rate (mean)	6.702	11. Unit bank dummy	.5574
1. Log total deposits (SMSA)	.3057		.52
	1.8949		1.22
	3.84a		.05
	.16	12. Account activity	.0396
2. Other services	−.2496		1.69
	.28		1.02
	3.29a		.04
	.14	13. Average deposit	−1.1145
3. Population increase	.0191		.0114
	6.60		.94
	3.16a		.04
	.13	14. Region 4	.1511
4. Concentration	.6835		.34
	.70		.93
	2.40b		.04
	.10	15. Region 5	.1464
5. Region 6	1.0482		.18
	.07		.90
	2.28b		.04
	.10	16. Log bank size	−.1006
6. Deposit fluctuation	.0790		2.0169
	1.76		.90
	1.98b		.04
	.08	17. Limited branch	
7. Other bank	−.1197	dummy	.3478
	.19		.41
	1.39		.79
	.06		.03
8. Region 3	−.1687	18. Time in debt	.0083
	.15		10.48
	1.35		.69
	.06		.03
9. Length of lending arrangement	−.0683	19. Region 2	−.0318
	2.59		.12
	1.35		.25
	.06		.01
10. Log original amount	−.0858	Intercept	5.372
	2.4583	R^2	.208
	1.29	F	7.75a
	.05	N	580

NOTE: See the notes to Table 2.

a Significant at the .01 level.

b Significant at the .05 level.

Appendix E

DISTRIBUTION OF CUSTOMERS

Appendix Table E-1

Customers Distributed by Region and Branching Restriction

	Region 1	Region 2	Region 3	Region 4	Region 5	Region 6	Total
All customers, branching law:							
Unit	0	46	226	1583	739	0	2594
Limited	1861	1121	868	165	191	0	4206
Statewide	190	0	120	0	0	504	814
Total	2051	1167	1214	1748	930	504	7614
No collateral, branching law:							
Unit	0	0	95	745	264	0	1104
Limited	1232	578	412	104	61	0	2387
Statewide	136	0	77	0	0	296	509
Total	1368	578	584	849	325	296	4000
100 per cent collateral, branching law:							
Unit	0	0	73	514	248	0	835
Limited	285	207	198	19	51	0	760
Statewide	8	0	2	0	0	124	134
Total	293	207	273	533	299	124	1729

Appendix Table E-2

Customers With Asset Data, Distributed by Region and Branching Restriction

	Region 1	Region 2	Region 3	Region 4	Region 5	Region 6	Total
All customers, branching law:							
Unit	0	19	158	1105	445	0	1727
Limited	1243	711	540	146	122	0	2762
Statewide	108	0	70	0	0	290	468
Total	1351	730	768	1251	567	290	4957
Nonsecured customers with data on assets, branching law:							
Unit	0	0	64	541	173	0	778
Limited	865	377	258	93	40	0	1633
Statewide	89	0	43	0	0	164	296
Total	954	377	365	634	213	164	2707
Fully secured customers with data on assets, branching law:							
Unit	0	0	41	332	141	0	514
Limited	137	98	108	15	34	0	392
Statewide	4	0	1	0	0	73	78
Total	141	98	150	347	175	73	984

Appendix Table E-3

Customers With Assets Less Than or Equal to $500,000, Distributed by
Region and Branching Restriction

	Region 1	Region 2	Region 3	Region 4	Region 5	Region 6	Total
All customers, branching law:							
Unit	0	10	95	587	277	0	969
Limited	756	472	254	65	76	0	1623
Statewide	78	0	41	0	0	157	276
Total	834	482	390	652	353	157	2868
Nonsecured customers, assets ≤ $500,000, branching law:							
Unit	0	0	23	189	91	0	389
Limited	530	231	120	42	29	0	952
Statewide	63	0	32	0	0	94	189
Total	593	231	187	299	126	94	1530
Fully secured customers, assets ≤ $500,000, branching law:							
Unit	0	0	23	189	91	0	303
Limited	81	72	61	6	16	0	236
Statewide	2	0	1	0	0	38	41
Total	83	72	85	195	107	38	580

Appendix Table E-4

Customers With Assets Greater Than $500,000 and Less Than or Equal to
$1 Million, Distributed by Region and Branching Restriction

	Region 1	Region 2	Region 3	Region 4	Region 5	Region 6	Total
All customers, branching laws:							
Unit	0	4	22	159	63	0	248
Limited	165	83	87	29	25	0	389
Statewide	14	0	8	0	0	53	75
Total	179	87	117	188	88	53	712
Nonsecured customers, assets $500,000 ≤ $1 million, branching laws:							
Unit	0	0	9	70	21	0	100
Limited	114	49	36	15	7	0	221
Statewide	11	0	5	0	0	23	39
Total	125	49	50	85	28	23	360
Fully secured customers, assets $500,000 ≤ $1 million, branching laws:							
Unit	0	0	9	63	22	0	94
Limited	17	13	18	3	9	0	60
Statewide	2	0	0	0	0	14	16
Total	19	13	27	66	31	14	170

Appendix Table E-5

Customers With Assets Greater Than $1 Million and Less Than or Equal to $5 Million, Distributed by Region and Branching Restriction

	Region 1	Region 2	Region 3	Region 4	Region 5	Region 6	Total
All customers, branching laws:							
Unit	0	5	29	198	65	0	297
Limited	190	89	117	39	18	0	453
Statewide	15	0	7	0	0	55	77
Total	205	94	153	237	83	55	827
Nonsecured customers, assets $1 million ≤ $5 million, branching law:							
Unit	0	0	15	89	32	0	136
Limited	124	56	54	27	3	0	264
Statewide	14	0	3	0	0	32	49
Total	138	56	72	116	35	32	449
Fully secured customers, assets $1 million ≤ $5 million, branching law:							
Unit	0	0	6	60	20	0	86
Limited	29	10	25	4	9	0	77
Statewide	0	0	0	0	0	17	17
Total	29	10	31	64	29	17	180

Appendix F

REGRESSIONS ON MODEL 4

Appendix Table F-1

Regressions on Model 4, All Customers With Asset Data, Three Size Classes, With a Six Partition Regional Variable, Mean Deposits Dependent

	Asset Size (millions of dollars)				
	$0 \le .5$		$.5 \le 1$		$1 \le 5$
Average deposit (mean)	118.29		373.94		773.15
1. Original amount	.0863	(3)	.0436	(1)	.1064
	346.51		1149.96		2579.41
	12.51[a]		3.04[a]		8.22[a]
	.23		.11		.28
2. Account activity	43.50	(1)	122.86	(2)	181.86
	1.79		2.07		2.20
	10.25[a]		6.45[a]		5.40[a]
	.19		.24		.19
3. Interest rate	−.3046	(4)	−.8447	(3)	−2.4596
	652.74		638.30		627.52
	4.77[a]		2.69[a]		3.43[a]
	.09		.10		.12
4. Log bank size	51.55	(2)	198.43	(4)	229.54
	6.0649		6.1443		6.1664
	4.75[a]		3.66[a]		2.07
	.09		.14		.07[b]
5. Length of lending arrangement	21.48	(18)	−3.69	(9)	88.88
	2.65		2.79		2.77
	3.50[a]		.10		1.30
	.07		.01		.05
6. Other services	30.66	(12)	19.54	(19)	2.28
	.23		.28		.30
	3.42[a]		.49		.03
	.06		.02		.01
7. Time in debt	−4.03	(17)	−1.52	(7)	−21.08
	9.95		10.56		10.29
	3.33[a]		.22		1.71
	.06		.01		.06
8. Unit bank dummy	−70.26	(10)	−67.16	(12)	−211.90
	.34		.35		.36
	2.90[a]		.55		.86
	.05		.02		.03
9. Region 4	43.09	(11)	−35.79	(8)	219.78
	.23		.26		.29
	2.61[a]		.50		1.58
	.05		.02		.06
10. Region 6	−65.10	(5)	−237.64	(13)	−214.20
	.05		.07		.07
	2.59[a]		1.93		.84
	.05		.07		.03

Appendix Table F-1—(*Concluded*)

	Asset Size (millions of dollars)				
	$0 \leq .5$		$.5 \leq 1$		$1 \leq 5$
11. Deposit fluctuation	10.72	(14)	6.61	(11)	46.14
	1.73		1.85		1.87
	2.39[b]		.31		1.10
	.04		.01		.04
12. Limited branch dummy	−42.68	(19)	−2.29	(16)	−38.00
	.57		.55		.55
	2.17[b]		.02		.17
	.04		.01		.01
13. Log total deposits (SMSA)	11.27	(15)	11.21	(10)	99.63
	5.9893		5.9990		6.0124
	1.29		.25		1.11
	.02		.01		.04
14. Region 5	−18.01	(9)	−51.98	(14)	−135.24
	.12		.12		.10
	1.04		.65		.82
	.02		.02		.03
15. Concentration	−28.97	(7)	−145.08	(6)	521.25
	.68		.68		.67
	.98		.96		1.79
	.02		.04		.06
16. Region 2	−10.66	(16)	−14.27	(17)	15.35
	.17		.12		.11
	.91		.22		.12
	.02		.01		.01
17. Population increase	.26	(13)	1.01	(5)	11.49
	7.36		7.26		7.02
	.40		.32		2.03[b]
	.01		.01		.07
18. Region 3	4.84	(6)	−60.62	(15)	34.49
	.14		.16		.19
	.38		1.01		.31
	.01		.04		.01
19. Other bank	2.27	(8)	−31.50	(18)	−7.31
	.14		.27		.42
	.21		.75		.10
	.01		.03		.01
Intercept	−149.98		−499.24		−863.44
R^2	.15		.16		.20
F	26.32[a]		6.92[a]		10.50[a]
N	2868		712		827

NOTE: See the notes to Table 2.

[a] Significant at the .01 level.

[b] Significant at the .05 level.

Appendix Table F-2

Regressions on Model 4, All Noncollateralized Customers With Asset Data, Three Size Classes, With a Six Partition Regional Variable, Mean Deposits Dependent

		Asset Size (millions of dollars)				
		$0 \leq .5$		$.5 \leq 1$		$1 \leq 5$
Average deposit (mean)		125.56		409.37		811.60
1. Original amount		.1312	(2)	.0631	(1)	.1598
		260.39		924.55		2285.81
		9.58[a]		2.92[a]		7.76[a]
		.24		.16		.35
2. Account activity		31.69	(1)	130.68	(2)	144.04
		1.82		2.14		2.21
		5.78[a]		5.58[a]		2.99[a]
		.15		.29		.14
3. Interest rate		−.4077	(5)	−1.0784	(5)	−2.1911
		648.44		627.15		621.68
		4.19[a]		2.02[b]		1.74
		.11		.11		.08
4. Log bank size		55.49	(4)	170.92	(18)	99.00
		6.1135		6.1854		6.1950
		3.91[a]		2.47[b]		.61
		.10		.13		.03
5. Deposit fluctuation		22.80	(19)	−.10	(16)	47.13
		1.74		1.89		1.86
		3.80[a]		.01		.76
		.10		.01		.04
6. Other services		33.60	(3)	126.44	(8)	118.99
		.20		.28		.33
		2.76[a]		2.57[b]		1.05
		.07		.14		.05
7. Length of lending arrangement		21.35	(18)	5.04	(11)	89.17
		2.67		2.82		2.77
		2.61		.10		.95
		.07		.01		.05
8. Time in debt		−3.39	(17)	.97	(12)	−15.23
		9.62		10.18		9.96
		2.26[b]		.13		.92
		.06		.01		.04
9. Region 6		−66.50	(14)	−35.85	(13)	297.80
		.06		.06		.07
		2.25[b]		.25		.92
		.06		.01		.04
10. Region 5		−46.58	(7)	−182.37	(9)	−266.36
		.08		.08		.08
		1.88		1.65		.98
		.05		.09		.05

Appendix Table F-2—(*Concluded*)

	0 ≤ .5		.5 ≤ 1		1 ≤ 5
			Asset Size (millions of dollars)		
11. Limited branch dummy	−31.28	(9)	150.00	(6)	418.24
	.62		.61		.59
	1.39		1.31		1.56
	.04		.07		.07
12. Other bank	−20.21	(8)	−76.36	(19)	33.16
	.11		.24		.42
	1.34		1.35		.32
	.03		.07		.02
13. Unit bank dummy	−26.65	(11)	134.32	(10)	311.96
	.25		.28		.30
	.88		.95		.95
	.02		.05		.05
14. Region 2	−12.46	(13)	−25.24	(17)	116.71
	.15		.14		.12
	.83		.34		.69
	.02		.02		.03
15. Log total deposits (SMSA)	8.04	(10)	56.22	(7)	159.51
	6.0856		6.0855		6.0842
	.73		1.04		1.30
	.02		.06		.06
16. Concentration	−26.50	(6)	330.46	(4)	728.41
	.66		.67		.66
	.67		1.72		1.79
	.02		.09		.09
17. Region 4	−13.88	(16)	16.12	(14)	163.63
	.20		.24		.26
	.62		.18		.82
	.02		.01		.04
18. Region 3	−9.32	(12)	−70.76	(15)	−128.85
	.12		.14		.16
	.56		.95		.79
	.01		.05		.04
19. Population increase	−.35	(15)	1.12	(3)	18.05
	8.06		7.83		7.30
	.40		.24		2.44[b]
	.01		.01		.12
Intercept	−98.55		−1026.07		−1316.03
R^2	.17		.25		.23
F	15.87[a]		6.07[a]		6.57[a]
N	1530		360		449

NOTE: See the notes to Table 6.
[a] Significant at the .01 level.
[b] Significant at the .05 level.

Appendix Table F-3

Regressions on Model 4, All Fully Collateralized Customers With Assets Less Than or Equal to $½ Million, With a Six Partition Regional Variable, Mean Deposits Dependent

Average deposit (mean)	113.52	11. Region 5	68.22
1. Account activity	75.03		.18
	1.69		1.19
	5.60[a]		.05
	.23	12. Interest rate	− .1254
2. Original amount	.0657		670.15
	551.84		.84
	4.82[a]		.04
	.20	13. Region 2	34.43
3. Region 4	160.01		.12
	.34		.77
	2.80[a]		.03
	.12	14. Population increase	− 1.40
4. Log bank size	103.43		6.60
	6.0169		.65
	2.63[a]		.03
	.11	15. Log total deposits	
5. Other services	69.70	(SMSA)	−18.20
	.28		5.89
	2.58[a]		.64
	.11		.03
6. Other bank	67.06	16. Unit bank dummy	−73.10
	.19		.52
	2.22[b]		.45
	.09		.02
7. Region 3	68.43	17. Deposit fluctuation	−2.96
	.15		1.76
	1.55		.21
	.07		.01
8. Length of lending arrangement	24.30	18. Region 6	23.50
	2.59		.07
	1.36		.14
	.06		.01
9. Concentration	−135.83	19. Limited branch dummy	2.03
	.70		.41
	1.34		.01
	.06		.01
10. Time in debt	−5.14	Intercept	−457.40
	10.48	R^2	.16[a]
	1.22	F	5.55
	.05	N	580

NOTE: See the notes to Table 6.

[a] Significant at the .01 level.

[b] Significant at the .05 level.

Index

Account activity in bank customer's profile data, 79–80

Assets, *see* Bank assets; Customer assets

Bank account activity, *see* Account activity

Bank assets:
of banks supplying customer profiles, 66–69
and economies of scale, 31

Bank compensation, sources of, 10, 56–57

Bank costs:
and geographical location of customer, 22
on loan, 12
of reduced return on assets, 13
See also Communication costs

Bank customers, *see* Customers

Bank deposits, *see* Demand deposits; Deposit size

Bank income:
and computation of customer profitability, 13–14
interest and deposit payments compared, 56n, 56–57

Banking regulations:
goals of, 1–2
and size of business, 23
See also Branching restrictions

Bank markets:
and branching restrictions, 2–3
competition in, 2
definition of, 21–24
estimation of performance of, 15
geographic delineation of, 23–24

and prices of bank services, *see* Price-structure relationship
SMSA definitions of, 40–41

Bank pricing, *see* Pricing decisions

Banks, compared with other enterprises, 7

Bank services, price of, *see* Price-structure relationship

Bank size:
and effect of deposit balances on interest rates, 49–50, 55
and loan rate, 30–31
and prices, 5
and price-structure relationship, 30–31, 59
and Regulation Q, 30
and supplying customer profiles, 66–69

Bargaining:
and bank prices, 15
and deposit balances, 20, 31

Bias, in bank customer profile data, 73

Borrowers, *see* Customers

Branching restrictions:
classes of, 2n
customers distributed by, 90–92
and customer profitability models, 16
and deposit balances, 55
and interest rates, 57–59
and loan rates, 43–44
and price-structure relationship estimates, 32–33, 37, 40
and structure of banking markets, 2–3

Business assets:
and price-structure relationship

99

Specification errors, and price-structure relationship estimates, 25

Tied-sale strategy, 8*n*

Uncollateralized customer regressions, 28, 31–32, 36